Conscious Living

EVOLVE CONSCIOUSLY

Anand Narayanan

notionpress.com

INDIA · SINGAPORE · MALAYSIA

ISBN 979-8-88833-313-6

Dedication:

This book is dedicated to my parents especially my mother who is no more with us. My Parents have been an inspiration in my life. Special thanks to my late mother for all that she taught me through her tolerance, composure, fortitude, fervent love, and modesty.

I am so grateful to have such parents who have made countless sacrifices to make sure their children get what they deserve. A big thank you to my sister for all the love and support that she has bestowed upon me. My gratitude to all my close friends, relatives, and family members who have constantly motivated and supported me in my journey.

All profits of this book go for the education, food, and medical expenses of underprivileged students of Care Foundation, Pune (Emmanuel Public School). I would be so grateful for your assistance in helping these kids.

Editor: Trupti Landage (Corporate Trainer and a Coach, NLP and Mindfulness Practitioner)

Contents

Foreword

"Anand is unique and talented. Rarely do you find an individual who is equally talented in business and spiritually. We normally think of the two as separate and unequal until you meet Anand. His calm demeanour pours out of every correspondence and communication. His breath of expert knowledge on spirituality is equally matched by his business IQ. The most impressive aspect of his character is that he's completely dedicated to helping others."
– **Willpower Harris (International Speaker, Business Coach, Best Selling Author and Humanitarian)**

Preface

I don't call myself a writer but someone who has a compelling message to share with the world that draws on my own life experiences, learnings, and inspiring tales and methods for growth and transformation. This book is the culmination of the six years of research I spent learning from numerous mentors, gurus, and teachers from around the world. I want to express my gratitude to all my mentors for their advice and the lessons I learned from them.

The reason for writing this book was to share my learning, "that transformation is possible without going through pain and suffering". From someone being entangled in bad habits, having no purpose in life, excessive stress, depression, compulsive thoughts and behaviours, and being financially broke to someone being able to live purposefully with financial freedom, clarity, fulfilment, happiness and peak performance is what I want to share with a wider audience. My goal is to inspire others think that everything is possible if I can do it.

Most people have been leading unconscious lives, without taking responsibility for what they truly want to achieve, create, have, be, experience, and contribute to this world. With conscious living, you will realize how to design the perfect life you desire, one that is clear, joyful, fulfilling, and at the top of your game. Recognize the factors influencing your current life and how you can change it using some frameworks, blueprints, and game-changing techniques that have been successful for millions of people.

The book will lead you through a step-by-step journey to discover how transformation happens and the elements that prevent us from moving forward in life. Recognize the significance of our belief systems, mindset, emotions, and life energies playing an important role in our overall development. Understand the different nuances and tricks relating to our body, mind, and emotions. Unfortunately, neither our schools nor universities provide us with any formal instruction or training on these important topics. Convenience and comfort have increased in today's digital, technological, and development-driven environment, but personal wellbeing has significantly diminished. We must now turn our attention inward because no quantity of outside goods or beings can bring us lasting enjoyment. Why do we always seek fulfilment and happiness outside of ourselves if they are both found within? Shouldn't we start exploring this life consciously? In this book, I've also discussed some of the spiritual and scientific frameworks, exercises and practices for inner well-being and unleashing your true potential.

Chapter 1

Introduction

I want to share a personal experience that inspired me to learn more about the interplay between the mind, body, emotions, and life energies. People frequently appear to be interested in learning more about my job life and how I happen to frequently travel to exotic places. How do I generate income? How do I fit in all this fun stuff? How do I handle things as an entrepreneur running a business? What's the secret, then? These are some of the enquiries I receive frequently.

I'd like to share the strategies I've learned from my mentors and applied in my own life that can help anyone function at their highest level while avoiding the difficulties associated with a lack of clarity, fulfillment, and satisfaction.

What does it take to get out of a rut and construct your life consciously? I'll have to briefly introduce myself to respond to this.

The year 2011 found me jobless, confused and broke. At 22 years old and a new MBA graduate, I was as lost in life just like most young people of my age are.

I had recently relocated to a new city where I knew nobody. I was out of a job, broke, and residing with my sister to save money on rent. I wasn't sure where to apply for jobs because I didn't have any clarity regarding my passions. My physique had little to no fitness despite playing numerous sports growing up. I was plagued with remorse over the decisions I had made in the past and my mind was always trying to ruin me. At the time, my girlfriend was a foreigner, which had its own set of difficulties because my parents did not support our relationship.

I was never in the present moment, constantly concerned about the future, filled with uncertainty and doubt. Strong urges sprang from all of this. The desire to travel, to be financially independent and to have the luxury of time to accomplish all the things I love while having every area of my life in congruence. I realised that I need to find a way to ignite the flame within myself to embark on the path of exploration.

After I completed my MBA, my college offered to position me at a reputable firm but I turned it down in favour of moving to Silicon Valley of India, Bangalore, where I hoped to find better employment opportunities. Unfortunately, nothing turned out to be as planned. I started working for a US-based company as a market research analyst, earning $150 a month. It didn't sound quite as cool as the designation suggested. Despite being paid a pittance, it was a dull, tedious work that provided absolutely nothing to fulfil me. However, I had a strong desire to learn new things and that led me to study more about the company and its different departments. I was intrigued by start-ups and my desire to learn how businesses functioned was what started me on my entrepreneurial journey. Just like every entrepreneur, I experienced many ups and downs every single day for a number of years.

Five years later, I once again hit rock bottom.

I was once more totally devastated.

I had 4 failed start-ups to my name.

I was now single.

Having bills to pay.

I was starting to consider getting a job again.

I was anxious, unhappy, and felt like a complete failure.

However, I still had some sense of resilience within me, that was the single quality that kept me going. In worst-case scenario, I planned to sell my car or get a part time job, but I had already made the decision that I will not give up entrepreneurship. I pursued my IT Company alone this time, this was my fifth venture. Although I had never done anything on my own and had always found partners to be very comforting, after four failed start-ups, I recognized I had to admit those partnerships were not the best options for me and were not working for them. I had made the decision to go into this endeavor alone. With an investment of $50 and some credit, I launched my fifth business and worked rigorously to attract clients. The biggest investment I put in this business was my time and energy for the first six months. I had seen a Ted talk by a speaker who revealed the secret of how to achieve Work-Life Balance which most people find difficult.

In his talk, the speaker emphasized the ideal quantity needed for an enjoyable lifestyle in India. He remarked, "In a city like Mumbai, it requires $3500 per month for a very good living for a single person." This occurred in 2016. Since I was stationed in Pune, which is a relatively affordable place to live, I was attempting to find out how to create an income of $2500 per month. I was now formulating my strategy to earn this sum with very little involvement while still living the lifestyle I sought, which included travelling, discovering, learning, and growing.

To cut a long tale short, I was able to achieve financial independence, time freedom, and the flexibility to pursue my passions within two years of launching my firm. I have been able to function while working 4-hour workweeks for a few years over the past six years. Now that I have all the systems and processes that are driving a healthy business for me, I can pursue everything I love. I want to reveal the secret I applied.

It was a 6-Step Method I Applied that I Learned from Napoleon Hill.

Steps:

1. Be incredibly passionate about getting what you want.

2. Identify precisely what you want to contribute in return to make it happen.

3. Establish a specific date by which you hope to fulfil or obtain your desires.

4. Establish a clear plan to put it into action.

5. Condense your goals into a clear statement that includes what you want, what you want to provide, when you want it accomplished, and how you propose to do it.

6. Recite your statement aloud twice a day with a visual that you already possess.

You must apply strategy, positive beliefs, resilience, and a strong desire that helped me achieve what I have today. These, however, are merely the surface-level elements and as you read through I will be deciphering the different aspects which can help you tap into the incredible capabilities of the mind. They enable you to access the mind's amazing potential, just like the way an athlete must practice every day vigorously to win the gold medal in the Olympics we have to practice the techniques religiously to see maximum benefits.

I was fortunate to travel across India and many other countries around the world to meet some of the most prominent and renowned speakers, entrepreneurs, and transformational coaches. During the last 6 years, I've had the opportunity to study the teachings of some of the top experts in the fields of yoga, spirituality, body, mind, and human performance.

Whatever you want can be manifested much more quickly, thanks to certain tools and techniques.

This book is designed to explore the methods I employed to get through the challenges in my life, which made me question if there are as many others as possible who could benefit from knowing these methods and secrets.

Freedom of Time and Wealth for Exploring Life

I struggled for a very long time to balance my time and money needs. Either I was broke and had plenty of free time, or I had enough money but no free time. Imagine being able to live a beautiful life with enough money and leisure for yourself. Everyone wants freedom, and I was no different. Prior to now, I wanted to advance professionally and succeed in a large organisation.

But as I gained knowledge and experience, I came to understand that the more you advance within a corporate organization, the more you fall into the wormhole and the less time you have for yourself. Being a part of such organizations you might enjoy the perks of paid business travel to other countries and other employee benefits however, these companies drain your energy and take away your freedom.It's fantastic if you enjoy what you do, but if you only do it for the paycheck, you will waste a significant portion of your life on worthless endeavours.

I was on a quest to come up with a system that would provide me more time and resources to experience life. I was struggling and puzzled as to what my true Dharma is. I was still unsure of what would bring me the greatest fulfillment and utmost happiness. I had to do some exploring for that, and one cannot do any exploring without time and money.

The vast majority of people on earth today are trapped in this cycle of working just for a pay check. They are caught in the loan they obtained for their residence, vehicle, or education. Their focus has shifted from fulfilment and happiness to making the most money possible. They have fears and limiting beliefs because they hold restrictive notions that their passion cannot provide them with a living. As a result of their pursuit, individuals are suffering from stress, anxiety, depression, and other mental, physical, and emotional traumas. Only when they crumble under the weight of grief or suffering do people understand they need to stop the rat race.

The majority of the people are in a race chasing after the things which they believe will lead to their success, but they are not pausing to think or even paying attention to what their soul is trying to tell them.

They have not discovered their true potential or their higher purpose. The ability of our minds to be influenced by things is quite easy to programme. Numerous individuals with busy schedules I've come across in my circle have expressed the desire to retire soon because of their unhappy lives. However, the expected soon never shows up, trapping them in a loop. Why should you soon retire is my query. Only if you dislike what you are doing, you may think of an early retirement. Would you ever decide to stop doing something you love? No right! There is no need to retire.

In the book Ikigai, it is said that there is no such thing as retirement in this Japanese village in Okinawa. This village is the most popular place in the world for its longevity because of its residents' sense of purpose and fulfilment in the work they love performing. Compared to other Japanese people, Okinawans have a 40% higher chance of surviving to 100, which is a significant factor in their extraordinary longevity. This village's residents are content, fulfilled, and driven by a sense of purpose.

In addition to sleep and chores, work takes up nearly 60 to 80 percent of our waking hours. Don't you believe our work should be meaningful, enjoyable, effective, and fulfilling to ourselves and others if it takes up such a large portion of our lives?

So, in my quest of finding the perfect blend of wealth and time, I started so many businesses and failed miserably on 4 occasions. My biggest challenge was I wanted to start a business with very little capital. In previous ventures, I never truly suffered a significant financial loss; rather, I merely lost time. However, I do consider those were some of the best years for learning, failing, and growing.

I ended my last business collaboration, a real estate partnership with a childhood pal. I had spent all my savings while I was involved in this venture, so I was back at square one. I was expecting payments from that firm, but I parted ways with it before I had a chance to open an account for it.

We were childhood friends and to me the relationship was more important than the wealth it brought. It was dreadful to hit rock bottom once again. I was driven by a strong desire to build a profitable company.

At that time in 2016, I launched a new firm from scratch with a $50 investment. I was unwilling to budge. Finally, the fifth venture was a success, and starting in 2016 up until this point in 2022, I have begun to experience a life of wealth and time.

I'm sharing this because starting something new from scratch is not difficult. Especially someone like me who had no prior business experience and lacked both the resources and the necessary understanding. Most people are afraid to quit their employment or family businesses and start something they love. They feel insecure and uncomfortable. They are constrained with a variety of limiting beliefs. I had realised that I had discovered the secret to my freedom of time and wealth that allowed me to explore so many new arenas. I started travelling to different places, meeting new people, and attending summits, workshops and conferences. I never stopped learning and was constantly upgrading myself, keeping the curiosity within me alive. I started exploring about peak performance, spirituality, body, mind and emotions from some of the world's leading gurus on the planet.

Our Education System is Flawed and is Consuming Up Our Creativity:

Even after spending more than 15 years in schools and colleges, we never learn anything about our body, mind, emotions, or life energy. We have been learning in order to get a degree and a certificate.

Each one of us is unique and we have our own individuality with varied potential. However, our current education system is not acknowledging this individuality and is trying to mould us all to match factory production standards. Only when we embrace our true expression and originality, will we be able to reach higher states of consciousness and create a major impact on this planet. It's said there is one thing which each one of us can do the best which nobody else on this planet can do. The question is have we embraced that within us?

According to the study conducted at the Carnegie Institute of Technology that 85% of your success comes from

- Your personality

- Your ability to connect with people

- Leadership and negotiating skills

Only 15% comes from our technical education. Despite this, there are some people spending an awful lot of money on things that are not even relevant. The education system that we are following was built for the industrial revolution age and we are still following the same. With the current advancements in AI and technology, AI will perform most of the tasks, and memorizing things is not going to be a test of intelligence anymore. We will have to start exploring the sides of real human intelligence and creativity. It's been said in yogic sciences that the intellect is useful for certain things while there are many other dimensions to the mind. There are deeper dimensions to the mind which are not being harnessed by our existing education system. It's like you trying to stitch a cloth with a knife. There are tools within our minds that can help us access deeper levels of consciousness and progress in this life effortlessly.

I am addressing a problem that majority of people are facing since our education systems have not shared the skills and knowledge for our mental, physical, emotional, and spiritual well-being. These are some of the most crucial abilities for boosting human potential, succeeding in life and creating positive impact in the society. My research and work gave me the opportunity to study the approaches and learn the methods and frameworks that millions of others have used to discover solutions. Success has different definitions and meanings for different people. However, reaching our full potential as humans will take us to the pinnacle. If we can do this, then achieving our goals in terms of income, health, and relationships will be simple. Achieving our greatest potential will enable us to experience the highest levels of fulfilment, happiness, and clarity of perception.

Primarily all people want is happiness and fulfilment. The goal is to master the skill of being at your best so that you can live every aspect of your life to the fullest. There is a strategy and a system for this, which I will discuss in this book. Being in the transformation sector I've had the privilege to work with some of the world's leading experts in the field of personal transformation, peak performance, and ultimate human performance.

In addition to being able to start travelling the world, I was also able to gain financial independence and have enough free time to experience life and be a lifelong learner.

Learning vs Transformation

Learning and transformation are not the same things. Learning can be done through reading, listening, or watching something. According to studies, you forget 80% of what you learned in just 24 hours. Therefore, learning is ineffective unless it follows a specific process. However, transformation functions differently. Transformation is an internal shift that brings us in alignment with our highest potential. Nothing of the old remains within you. Your thoughts feelings and actions are newly aligned. It is a shift in your life energies or consciousness that changes the way you perceive and live in this world. Transformation is comparable to a rose blooming from a plant that is covered with thorns. If you've ever seen a rose plant it's full of thorns but yet it's admired for its beauty despite all the thorns. The image of the rose blooming from those thorns is an analogy for transformation.

Transformation Happens in 2 Scenarios

1. **Pain or Suffering**
2. **Growth Mind-set**

Transformation due to Pain or Suffering:

"The wound is the place where the light enters" – Rumi

Someone experiencing severe health conditions suddenly realizes and learns how important it is to look after their body.

Someone who has gone through a bad relationship understands what they are looking for in a companion.

Someone who has had a terrible boss realizes entrepreneurship is such a blessing.

People only decide to make positive changes in their lives after going through pain and suffering. Individuals who go through this form of transformation generally evolve slowly depending on the insights and wisdom they acquire by chance or depending on the level of suffering they encounter. Since they are not consciously seeking wisdom for growth they don't have any accelerated growth. Their progress, however, can be exponential if they have a growth attitude and have experienced hardship.

Think of an incident in life that caused you to experience pain or suffering and led you to a turning point in life!

Transformation due to Growth Mindset:

When we inculcate a growth mindset one can consciously evolve with knowledge, methods and practices. You don't have to undergo suffering or wait to experience pain. This is a wonderful way for transformation and growth.

A growth mindset will make you spend time with the right people that inspire you or help you grow.

It will develop your mind to have empowering thoughts.

It will lead you to take positive actions towards your goals.

It will instil the right habits and values essential for your growth.

It will encourage you to learn from teachers and have the right mentors.

A growth mindset is required to have transformation in every area of your life.

A growth mindset works perfectly with certain practices which can enhance the transformation process.

In the growth mindset, it's crucial to follow certain guidelines.

There are 7 aspects that need to be combined for your Transformation Process that I learned from Vishen Lakhiani, the author of the book "Code of the Extraordinary Mind". These practices have to be combined with each other for transformation to take place. These procedures are used by every top transformation coach, mentor, or guru to help you transform.

1. Creating New Models of Reality

Our lives are continually shaped by our beliefs, values, and perceptions. Only when the existing models of reality are destroyed, and new conscious ones are created will we be able to make transformation possible.

We begin to create a shift at every step when we become conscious of our values, beliefs, and the interpretations we give to various situations and facets of life.

2. Creating Systems of Living

Do you follow any successful habits and routines or are you just zipping each day as it comes? Once you create new models of reality it's important to have systems, habits, and practices to abide by on a daily basis. You cannot expect to build muscles without working out. In the same way, you cannot expect transformation without having systems, methods and practices. If we consciously don't choose our habits, they will end up choosing us.

3. Critical Reflection

According to the University of Toronto critical reflection is the number one thing that creates transformation. Critical reflection is a "meaning-making process" that aids us to set goals, apply what we've learned in the past to update future actions and considering the real-life implications of our thinking. It serves as a bridge between thinking and doing, and most effective, it can be transformative.

If your mentor asks you what did you learn from your setback yesterday? To this question, you would have a reflection. However, if you want to do a critical reflection your mentor would have to ask you "what have you realised you've been missing or doing wrong since yesterday.

Journaling would be valuable to put up your thoughts. "Writing in a journal each day allows you to direct your focus to what you accomplished, what you are grateful for and what you are committed to doing better tomorrow. Thus, you more deeply enjoy your journey each day" - Hal Elrod

Studies show that critical reflection can have a direct impact on motivation and performance levels.

4. Consuming Rich Content

Watching, listening or attending a documentary or a talk that is inspiring, and knowledgeable or a discussion that is enlightening, and information that can make you change and creates a shift within you would be considered rich content.

It spurs you to take action. However only consuming this content will not guarantee transformation and it needs to be combined with other aspects of transformation practices too.

5. Community

We are social beings, and we connect with stories. The very concept of a community establishes a forum for inspiration and sharing. One of the best ways you can teach, learn and share with each other is through community. According to the study we retain information best when we teach it to someone else and the second best when we discuss it with others. A community becomes a great platform to execute this and always keeps you driven.

You can be part of communities on WhatsApp, Facebook, LinkedIn, Quora, clubs, societies and so many more online and offline communities. Depending on your objective it's best to be part of communities that help you have a sense of belonging and create a safe place for you to express, discuss, connect, and grow.

6. Meditation and Breathworks

There are 4 practices that let you tap into altered states of the mind.

1. Meditation

2. Breath works

3. Neuro training

4. Plant medicine

Plant medicine is a drug and is an external stimulant out of these. It involves a lot of purging and has to be done under the guidance of a shaman. Also there is no assurance if the person will have a positive experience or no. While some people have gone into really bad states while some have experienced wonderful states. Some have managed to transform on many levels just with one sitting, however it's unpredictable. Plant medicine is not the ideal technique to achieve altered states because it is hazardous, unsustainable, and unreliable.

Neurotraining costs a lot of money and necessitates a lot of equipment.

Hence, out of the four, meditation and breath exercises are the most trustworthy, practical, and long-lasting remedies.

Meditation and breath work have the power to

1. Heal emotional trauma and pain.

2. Increase Self Awareness.

3. Reprogram the Mind.

4. Overcome Addictions.

5. Overcome Stress and Anxiety levels.

6. Increase levels of focus and concentration.

7. Increase joy and happiness.

8. Align your energies.

9. Creative Visualisation for manifesting goals and a lot more.

Meditation and breath works play an important role in the transformation and these practices work on body, mind, emotions and life energies.

7. Application

Having a list of tasks to accomplish from your learning is absolutely necessary. Whatever you learn, needs to be applied practically for the learnings to materialize.

When your learnings are put into practice, your confidence and sense of accomplishment are boosted.

We are frequently more motivated to reach the goal when we make progress and see things getting done. Therefore, as soon as you learn something, put it to use right away.

The combination of these 7 activities is exactly what is needed for our transformation and to reach peak performance.

Journey of Exploration and Curiosity

I was raised in a spiritual family where my grandfather was a spiritual leader at an organization called Shri Ram Chandra Mission (also known as Heartfulness) which is established in over 150 countries and promotes the practice of heart-fullness meditation. Even after receiving initiation from my grandfather when I became 18 years old, I was not inclined toward spirituality. I had no idea what a blessing it was to have a family member who was such a well-known spiritual teacher around the world. At that age, I didn't truly understand its significance and thought it uninspiring. Like many others, I was initially sceptical and found it difficult to accept the idea that someone could heal you or transmit energy. It was completely above my rationality, and the logical mind frequently dismisses anything that doesn't make sense.

The logical mind needs constant scientific validation. No one ever provided any interesting scientific evidence or demonstrated it to me, for me to actually comprehend the significance of meditation at that time. I therefore never had a strong desire to pursue it. But approximately ten years later, when I was 28 and living life, my interest in this realm grew. We all have a desire to grow and a desire for more from life. This is a characteristic of human nature. I started exploring the mystical sides of reality. Something drove me and I developed a longing for the truth. I was curious to know more. I wanted answers to so many of my questions. I refrained from just believing in something that I was told to believe. I was muddled in my own psychological dramas of the mind and its patterns that ruined my perception and clarity towards life. Every single one of us believes, feels, or senses that there is something bigger than ourselves. It's only when we pay attention to the surroundings and ourselves we understand how perfect this universe is and how brilliantly it is functioning for millions of years. There is perfection in everything, whether you look at a bug or a flower, it is incredible. Our human mechanism itself is so sophisticated that we haven't explored it in its entirety.

My biggest epiphany came from Sadhguru, an Indian yoga master and spirituality advocate. He proclaimed, "that we are not our bodies nor our mind". Then I became even more curious, and I found it difficult to process these facts. We have been so conditioned to connect with our physical, emotional, and psychological selves that I truly struggled to understand them.

I was so fascinated by this that I found it difficult to sleep for several days. This triggered my interest in our mind, body, life forces, and emotions. I registered for a couple of professional-led workshops. After much research and my personal experiences, I've come to the realization that we are not our physical or mental selves. They merely serve as our tools for us to experience this life. Your mind is nothing more than a collection of impressions and information gathered from your senses, while your body is something you have accumulated from this world. Although they could be yours, they couldn't be you.

A highly renowned Neurosurgeon who was a specialist on the brain and well known for his understanding and knowledge of the different parts of the brain had performed various experiments. One of his most well-known experiments involved activating a patient's motor cortex as the patient's arm began to move upward as a result. The surgeon asked him are you moving your arm upwards? The patient said "no", it's moving on its own. Now, the doctor instructed him to wilfully transfer it to the other side, which he did. The surgeon was making an effort to locate the commander of the choice.

Thus, the surgeon was able to track the command's origin in the brain but he was unable to track the commander from where it came for execution. Until today, there has been no technology that is able to track the location of the commander that we call soul or life. No matter what sophisticated gadget these surgeons have at their disposal, they are unable to identify the decision-maker who ordered the hand to move. The body that will carry out those orders is chosen by the commander. This live demonstration illustrates that we are not our bodies or minds.

We are so controlled by our physical and psychological selves that we actually end up believing that's us. Most of us are being controlled by the compulsive states of our body and mind. Our behaviours and actions can be on autopilot mode. Someone who has become habituated to a particular programme is the cause of their feelings of rage, envy, anguish, hatred, and fear. One can choose to be in a positive state if they are not a victim of this program. You always have the choice to be conscious and that is the real you. The mind only creates patterns and programmes that will eventually lead you into endless circles. You keep getting stronger at the things you practise, and those patterns become ingrained. The emotions you consciously or unconsciously create have a significant role in determining how you feel and what experiences you have in life. Most people have a set of subconscious emotional states that are pre-programmed to either make them happy or sad, furious or calm, worried or relaxed, and so on. The quality of our lives is determined by our capacity to intentionally design them.

Consider the following scenario and attempt to picture yourself there. You are the most significant participant at this meeting, yet you are running late. As you navigate the streets, you eventually get to a spot where there is a tremendous traffic jam. It's 40 degrees C outside and a prime summer afternoon. Your car breaks down suddenly now. You are attempting to diagnose the issue with your car while it is blazing hot outside. When a homeless man approaches you and requests food or money, you become enraged and decline to assist him. Someone runs into you on the sidewalk while attempting to get somewhere. Due to your extreme agitation, you yell at your spouse over the phone when they were merely attempting to assist you. You experience a string of awful emotional states. If I were to describe the history of each of these persons and mention that the beggar had not eaten for three days and was responsible for feeding a 6-year-old who was at risk of starving. The individual who ran into you was in route to the hospital to see his dying mother, who might not have survived if he arrived later. Your spouse just needed little encouragement after finishing a long day of domestic responsibilities. Wouldn't your anger disappear after I told you this information? With each of them, you would not have reacted in the same manner. The takeaway is that you are ultimately responsible for creating your mental state and behaviour, and you have total power over both. When you respond to them negatively, it starts a chain reaction of bad things happening to them not only the negative emotional reaction you gave people.

We only become conscious when we switch from a reactive to a responsive attitude. If we can be conscious at this moment and create peace, then aren't we capable of creating the next moment also the way we want? If we can look at life only one moment at a time, then our life can be the way we want, and our conscious living journey can begin.

Chapter 2

Beliefs: Foundation of Our Life

Foundation of a Personality

"Your beliefs become your thoughts, your thoughts become your words, your words become your actions, your actions become your habits, your habits become your values, and your values become your destiny." – Mahatma Gandhi

Just like in a computer you have the Operating System which is the most important software that manages all the hardware and software of the computer, same goes with beliefs that manage the body, mind, and emotions.

Something which was told by Mahatma Gandhi has been mentioned by numerous other leaders, gurus, and people in the field of the study of science and spirituality.

Who we are today is nothing but an accumulation of the beliefs and identities we gathered over time. These beliefs are constantly controlling our life whether we are conscious or unconscious of it.

The Cycle of Destiny

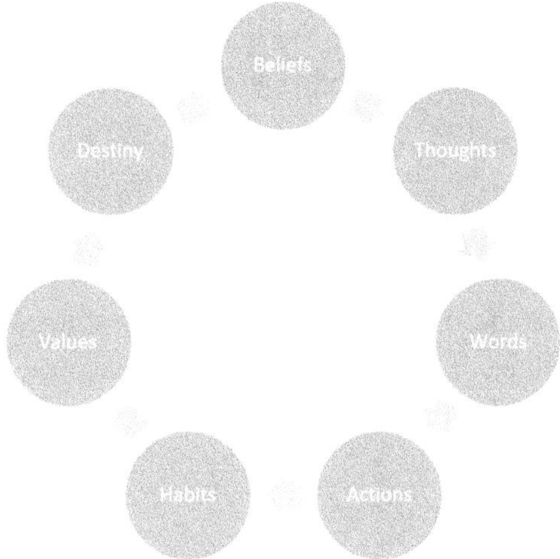

In this complex world to make sense of things our intellect filters all experiences and sets beliefs about everything. These beliefs have been happening consciously and unconsciously. Unfortunately, with most people, it happens unconsciously.

"Whether you think you can or think you can't you're right." - Henry Ford

An avid traveller once visited an elephant camp, and he was surprised to see a full-grown giant elephant chained to a piece of rope. To his curiosity, he asked one of the trainers how-come the elephant can't break through a rope-like this and escape? To which the trainer replied "When they were very young and much smaller, they were tied up with the same size rope and it was good enough to hold them back then. As a result, the elephant has developed to believe that he cannot break free from the rope and makes no attempt.

The only reason the elephant was still there was that it was conditioned to believe that it is impossible to break free from that rope.

Moral of the Story:

Your beliefs will be the main factor influencing your behaviour and the outcomes you achieve. The elephant in this situation has been trained since childhood to believe that he is not powerful enough to burst open from the rope that is holding him back, even though he is more than capable of escaping from that rope.

Years of such conditioning forced me to battle to accept the beliefs that society, my instructors, parents, my friends, and my experiences as a child lead me to believe.

Unconsciously, those beliefs were controlling how I lived. I became aware of the blueprint of beliefs that were in control of my life and realized I had to act right away to prevent my beliefs from continuing to steer me away from the life I want to live.

I realized to change my life, I had to change my beliefs. I had unlocked a big secret, all I needed to do was figure out how to swap out my old, restricting beliefs with new, empowering ones.

Unfortunately, the most crucial events that mould our personalities and futures just occur to us unconsciously. Everyone experiences this, but only a small percentage of people intentionally choose their beliefs. I came to the realisation that I needed to deliberately form these beliefs and those that will give me strength. We continually form views about everything, a number of which are based on prior experiences, a portion of which are handed down from one generation to the next, others of which come from our friends, some of which come from society, and so on.

We keep constructing such beliefs based on past experiences. You gave your lover your complete love and devotion, only to learn that one day, they left you for someone else.

You lose trust in all men/women. You generalise them by claiming that men/women can't be trusted. Now with this belief being engrained in your mind, it continues to provide you with more of these scenarios, and your belief will cause you to perceive and draw conclusions based on those perceptions. Now, even if the right person enters your life, your belief will prevent you from committing to anything long-term. Your conclusion is that he or she cannot be relied upon.

You might not be aware of this belief, but your thoughts, words, actions, habits, and values would have already changed based on it, and they are ultimately leading to the outcome. Your personality gets formed by your beliefs. Your beliefs shape your personality.

This led me to a stage when I had to unlearn everything and start over. It was a process of dissolving. I was excited to have discovered the key to altering my core set of identities. I discovered several methods for reprogramming my subconscious mind, which I will discuss subsequently. Additionally, if you practice the approach, you will discover how to transform your limiting beliefs into ones that will help you realise your goals and manifest what you desire.

How Do We Get Conditioned to Our Beliefs?

Primary Methods of Learning and Conditioning

1. **Verbal Programming** – What did you hear when you were young. Beliefs about wealth may take the form of something similar to the below listed examples:

   1. Money doesn't grow on trees.

   2. Save your money for a rainy day.

   3. It takes a lot of money to make money.

   4. You need money to be successful.

   5. Money doesn't bring happiness.

   6. Money doesn't bring love.

   7. You have to work really hard to make money.

8. We can't afford it.

9. Wealthy people are dishonest.

10. We don't have enough money.

These above statements are examples of the beliefs we hold in our subconscious. The worst aspect is that it is taking place subconsciously on us without our knowledge. Similar to how our careers and relationships are shaped, our interactions with others, our health, and other aspects of our lives are also shaped by blueprints.

2. **Modelling** – What did you see when you were young?

   What were your parents like financially?

   What were your grandparents, neighbors relatives, and teachers like?

   Would they spend lavishly or economically?

   Did they have limiting beliefs about money?

   Did they have beliefs of lack or abundance towards money?

   Unless you work on altering your views, you will only be like one of them or a blend of some.

3. **Specific Incidents** – What did you experience?

   Did you ever go through hard times or experience being broke?

   Did you struggle with money, or was there an abundance of it?

   When parents fight over money it can leave scars on the child's subconscious about wealth.

Belief Blueprint Change Process

The process for changing your blueprint is quite simple. However, it requires reprogramming your subconscious mind with the repetition of thoughts, words, and emotions.

Steps:

- Identify your beliefs

- Acknowledge and accept

- Switch with Empowering Beliefs

Identify Your Beliefs

We don't have a conscious mind until we are 7 years old. That is why it is common to witness children always in a state of unconditional joy and ecstasy. Only their subconscious mind is in action while they are in the delta, theta and alpha stages. It's comparable to feeding a new smartphone with all software or like a blotting paper that will absorb all the liquid you feed. It will take in anything that is put into it without discriminating between good and bad. For this reason, it is said that instilling the proper values and beliefs in them while they are still young is of core importance.

Most of their beliefs are mostly programmed at this age. If you were hypothetically born into Bill Gates' family, wouldn't you believe that "Money is Abundant and Comes Easy"? However, if you were raised in a low-income home, you can have the exact opposite set of views. After the age of seven, repetition helps to shape all beliefs. 95% of life is controlled by our subconscious mind, which is quite powerful.

Our conscious mind can process around 40 bits of information per second while our subconscious brain can manage around 11 million bits of information per second. So, you can understand how much more potent our subconscious mind is compared to our conscious part of the brain. We aren't even aware that the thoughts that have been ingrained in our brains either come from our early years or have been reinforced via repetition. Consider how you first learnt to ride a bike. It would have been difficult for you to balance and maneuver your first-time riding.

However, with constant practice, it gets implanted into your subconscious and you eventually get to a point where riding is quite simple. You would also notice that once it's consumed into your subconscious you would effortlessly go from point A to B with ease. Depending on one's capabilities we can train our subconscious to a level where it can work in our favour. One of the biggest tools to accelerate growth in our life is strong beliefs in alignment with our life vision and destiny.

It is very important to first identify our beliefs in relation to a certain aspect and then introspect whether they functioning in our favour or against us. Let's take the example of a hypothetical belief that one can have. The people who frequently ask, "Why does this keep happening to me?". Those are the people who believe they are unlucky. They are the ones who think nothing goes their way. They are the ones who consider life as a dreadful thing. Even when many things don't go in our favour but not everyone believes in bad luck. Now, a person who has those beliefs might not express them however they possess those beliefs. I am sure you probably know someone in your network who holds such beliefs. You will see they actually cause harm to themselves. They just aren't aware of how their habitual behaviours control their life. What do you anticipate the repercussions of such beliefs would be? The root cause for various consequences is the beliefs we hold. Their negative beliefs bring negative thoughts which turn into negative words. These words turn into negative actions and when those actions are repeated frequently, they tend to develop into bad habits. Once these habits are performed regularly it becomes their personality and a part of their values. Now the mind is completely programmed to these values and that leads them to their negative destiny.

I was aware if I wanted to change my life, I had to soon identify the limiting beliefs and swap them with empowering ones. I had limiting beliefs about wealth, health, relationships, career, business, and personality. The goal is to examine your views in detail regarding each aspect of your life.

How to Identify Limiting Beliefs?

1. List down your beliefs

Write down the beliefs in every area of your life. When you list them down you get complete clarity on the beliefs which are actually limiting and the ones that are empowering you.

2. Behaviour Based

Take note of your unfavorable behavior in specific situations. If you reflect on the instances where you acted adversely and analyse them, you will find that a certain limiting thought was the cause for it. For instance, if you don't speak English very well and are around a lot of new people, you might not say anything. You may hold the self-esteem-related view that "I'm not good enough." You are concerned that others will judge you and that you might be shamed or made fun of. Your subconscious tells you that you are inadequate.

3. Outcome-based

If you have been struggling in certain aspects of your life like finances, health, or relationship. Just find out the challenges you have, and the belief associated with that challenge. For instance, if wealth is something that you have been struggling with, then ask yourself the beliefs you have about wealth.

Try this little exercise to uncover some of your limiting beliefs about wealth.

1. Being rich requires ______________________________

2. I am not financially free because______________

3. I'd love to have more money but______________

4. Rich people are______________

It's possible that you have empowering beliefs about money which has brought prosperity in your life. You may not always have limiting beliefs however, there could be a couple of them which still might be existing and hinder further growth. Also, if you identify your empowering beliefs, you can repeat such beliefs in every area of your life.

My Limiting beliefs about Wealth were:

"Being rich requires a lot of hard work"

"It takes a lot of money to start a business"

"Rich people are unethical"

"Rich people are unhappy and stressed out"

Exercise: Identify the limiting beliefs about your

1. Social relationships (Friends, relatives, colleagues, etc)

2. Love relationships (Family and your love partner)

3. Career or Business (Purpose, passion, paycheck, etc)

4. Finances (The way you deal, use and believe about money)

5. Life Vision (Your goals, the things you want to experience in life, how you want to grow in life, how you want to contribute in life.)

6. Parenting (What it means to you)

7. Health (Your ideal self, workout, sports, games, fitness)

8. Spirituality (Meditation, peace, religion)

9. Mental Factors (Your thoughts, ideas, attitude, mindset etc.)

10. Intellectual Factors (Things that enhance your Creativity and are mentally stimulating)

11. Emotional States (The states you often reside in)

Identify limiting beliefs in every area of your life. Once you have completed this exercise, which could take some time, you can shape the life you want by embedding new beliefs which are empowering. Now that you know the power of beliefs you can make the empowering ones more powerful if you think they are not strong enough.

Acknowledge and Accept

Once you are done identifying your limiting beliefs, you must acknowledge and become aware of them. Without becoming aware of these beliefs, they cannot be changed. An alcoholic can never quit alcohol if he doesn't accept that he is an alcoholic. So, accept you're limiting beliefs and understand how these limiting beliefs are holding you back from reaching your potential. It gets simpler to let things go once you embrace them and become aware of them.

Switch with Empowering Beliefs

After you identify, acknowledge, and accept your limiting beliefs you have to swap them with an empowering belief. When we as humans choose unhelpful beliefs and do nothing to change them, we eventually wind up living like an elephant that has been taught to believe he is weak and is unaware of his true potential.

By keeping our limiting ideas in the present tense, we can teach our subconscious that they are already real and replace them with empowering ones. Now here is an important aspect of doing it right. What you want is not fulfilled. You get what you feel and what you are. The real trick lies in the emotions you put in. It has to be said like you mean it, with emotions.

"Being rich requires a lot of hard work" replaced with → "I am rich even with the least effort"

I must mean it when I say, "I am rich even with the least effort," and not simply say it. It won't work if I claim to be wealthy while still feeling broke and underprivileged. I was therefore telling the universe—or vibrating at a frequency that was indicating that if I don't work hard, I don't deserve to be rich—when I held the concept that being wealthy needs a lot of hard effort. Many people put in a lot of effort, yet they haven't seen the desired results. So, achieving wealth or success requires more than just hard work—it also requires a firm belief in your words, deeds, and a burning desire for your goals. Even the hardest-working security guard or construction worker won't become wealthy just with hard work. So, what makes you think this way? If Mark Zuckerberg and my security guard were compared, my security guard would likely put in more effort. Therefore, there shouldn't be any connection between wealth and hard work. When I changed my belief, I was able to earn ten times more with one-fifth the amount of work I would put in. It is unbelievable how things can transform with some small foundational changes.

"It takes a lot of money to make money" replaced with → "I don't need much money to make a lot of money"

Dhirubhai Ambani, a rags-to-riches story, built Reliance Industries in Mumbai after beginning his career at a gas station. He used to borrow money, incur losses, and split profits when he won because he had no money at all to trade with. Ambani took Reliance Public in 1977, and at the time of his demise, he was valued $25.6 billion. He had neither received significant support from anyone nor was he wealthy when he first started. If we alter our thoughts, anyone can accomplish what he did. He possessed a great burning desire and passion to grow into a huge man, which was supported by strong beliefs. Naturally, he was successful due to a variety of other circumstances, but his beliefs have always been the most important. There are countless case studies of people who have accomplished a great deal by possessing particular beliefs.

"Rich people are evil and unethical" replaced with → "Rich people are virtuous and ethical"

I had seen some wealthy people in the past who were immoral and wicked, and I generalised this to believe that all wealthy people are like this. However, not all wealthy people are dishonest or bad. My subconscious prevented me from being wealthy while I was clinging to that belief. Even if I have money, I can choose to be moral and upright. I then changed my outlook and began to follow those who possessed a high degree of morality and virtue.

"Rich people are unhappy" replaced with → "Rich people are happy"

I had the impression that those who were wealthy were generally miserable and had many challenges. This notion kept me from becoming wealthy. It started to form inside of me as I observed the strained relationships, fights, and monotonous lives of wealthy people. But as you may be aware, a great deal of people also have great fortune and are equally happy in life.

"Money is not spiritual" replaced with → "Money is the highest form of Spirituality"

I did not feel that money is spiritual because I come from a spiritual household and watched my grandfather perform social service by teaching meditation to numerous individuals for free. And I've always wanted to pursue spirituality in the same way as my grandfather. I was so unconsciously preventing my financial growth. Because I could do so many good things in the form of charity if I had a lot of money,

I modified my thinking to "Money is the highest form of spirituality." It's heart-breaking to see people who have a desire to contribute but don't appear to have a lot themselves, I therefore began working for a greater goal, which started motivating me to become wealthy and earn more money.

I had so many limiting beliefs regarding money.

"Making money is incredibly difficult."

"There aren't enough ways to make money,"

"Rich people are greedy"

I'm sure you would resonate with me on some of my beliefs and it turns out that our beliefs shape the world in which we live.

- Only if I work hard, I can be wealthy.

- Only if I am good-looking, I can get the desired love partner.

- Only if I get that (gadget, job, love, money, etc) I will be happy.

And so on…

If we consider these as our beliefs hypothetically then we could change them to empowering beliefs like

- I can be wealthy with limited efforts.

- I can get the desired love partner regardless of who I am."

- Happiness needs no reason, and I am happy without any reason.

The time required for changing your limiting beliefs to empowering ones depends on how deeply your beliefs are ingrained. The deeper the beliefs are instilled in your subconscious the longer will it take for you to alter these beliefs.

How do you replace these beliefs with empowering ones?

You must replace limiting beliefs using your

1. Thoughts

2. Words

3. Emotions

Some of the best practices are:

- Affirmations

- Incantations

- Asking Yourself Empowering Questions

Affirmations

Affirmations are nothing but positive statements that can help you overcome negative and self-sabotaging thoughts by helping you reprogram your beliefs. When repeated often with an emotional intensity you will start seeing positive changes in your beliefs and thoughts. You will feel the difference in your energy just by saying these affirmations. The more loudly you say it and with emotional intensity, the faster you can program your subconscious mind.

It is best when you say your affirmations starting with an "I am" as it's in the present tense.

For example:

I am grateful for the family I have.

I am always at the right place at the right time.

I am constantly being offered new opportunities for success.

I am a money magnet and attract money very easily.

I am proud of my decisions.

I am now a reflection of my highest self.

I am a beautiful person inside and out.

I am loving myself more and more every day.

I am worthy of connections that are loving, caring, and genuine.

I am an ever evolving and ever-expanding person

I am always surrounded by love.

I attract everything easily and effortlessly.

You can look in the mirror and say it aloud with emotional intensity or you can just say it in a place you are comfortable. Although, you can say it in your mind, but speaking it aloud has better and faster results. When you speak anything out loud, deeper vibrations are created which are then released, and they start manifesting in the physical world. Try to observe this when you say it loud, you can immediately feel an energy shift and you will feel much more empowered. The universe responds to your frequency. So, when you start a practice of saying these empowering beliefs aloud with emotional intensity you are not only sending out positive frequency but also programming your subconscious with new beliefs.

We cannot rewire our subconscious by repeating something a few times. The subconscious mind will take us seriously when we provide regular assurance. Our subconscious is responsible for numerous automatic processes like our heartbeat, blood flow, digestion, breathing, and many other bodily functions. They take place automatically. So, if we want our subconscious to run our beliefs on autopilot, we must apply this practice for at least 30-60 days depending on the kind of emotional intensity you put forth. Remember that emotional intensity is vital here and it must appear to be already real.

Often these limiting beliefs have been so deeply ingrained that it must be reinforced in your subconscious with repetition. Just the way you learned the English alphabet, we must continue with it repeatedly. However, if they are implanted in your subconscious, the new ideas will begin influencing your thoughts, words, behaviors, habits, values, and future.

Incantations

Incantations are like spoken prayers that are similar to mantras, that are to be said aloud. The difference between affirmation and incantation is that incantation is a lot with emotional intensity and saying it aloud. However, affirmations may or may not be done with emotional intensity or with a high pitch. As a result, incantations are much more effective and powerful in comparison to affirmations.

Asking Yourself Empowering Questions

This is a highly powerful technique that works wonders in challenging our minds to assist us to evolve and grow. In this strategy, you ask yourself empowering questions to oneself like:

1. How are you so confident and charismatic?

2. How do you generate income so easily?

3. How do you stay so fit?

When you repeat this every day, something extremely interesting consequently occurs. The subconscious mind is incapable of distinguishing between reality and fiction. When you keep asking yourself these questions, your subconscious mind starts to believe that you are telling the truth. For instance, if you've been wondering how you're so fit.

Your subconscious believes that you are already physically fit. This automatically triggers a change in your thoughts, words, actions, habits, and values which gets you to your desired output. So always ask questions that are empowering. The opposite is also possible and can hamper negative growth.

For example, if you ask yourself a disempowering question like

Why am I so fat? Your mind answers back saying because you're a pig.

This not only makes your subconscious believe you are fat but also creates a chain of negative thoughts, which lead to a negative chain of words, actions, habits, and values and eventually lead you to a negative output. So, asking yourself empowering questions is a game-changer and can change the discourse within yourself.

Effects of Beliefs on Our Physical Body

"Drugs are not always necessary, [but] belief in recovery always is."

– Norman Cousins

Norman Cousins in his novel "Anatomy of an Illness" explains his rigorous recovery from Ankylosing spondylitis, a painful collagen illness that made him immovable and nearly incapable of moving his jaw. His doctor and a close friend clearly explained to him that just one out of every 500 patients who receive this treatment truly recovers. This put Norman on a pursuit to learn the cause of how his body was responding and how he could undo this harm. He went into his flashback to understand what got him into this state, he figured out and arrived at a conclusion that his recent trip to Russia got him in this state. His trip to Russia was extremely stressful which led to weak immunity and him getting exposed to harmful fumes of diesel trucks round the clock. He figured out that he had to reinstate his immune system and he began to figure out how?

He discovered that negative emotions like rage, worry, self-doubt, and envy are connected to adrenal depletion from Hans Selye's book "Stress of Life." He, therefore, reasoned that the opposite would be true and that beneficial outcomes would be produced by pleasant emotions like love, laughter, faith, and appreciation.

For his immunity and discomfort, 38 medications were prescribed to him. Upon realising how harmful it was, he asked the doctor to just prescribe Vitamin C for his immunity, and to ease his pain, he turned to comedies like the Marx Brothers films. Candid Camera includes selections from the subtreasury of American humor by EB & White. He realized that 10 mins of laughter would produce about 2 hours of pain-free sleep.

The result of his laughter therapy was pretty clear. Within a couple of years, he was completely pain-free, though he continued to take vitamin C for his immunity. He mentally cured his condition with an overlooked laughter therapy to live to the age of 75 with no medication. Therefore, with the power of your mind, you can recover with unconventional methods.

In one of Norman's interviews, he shared a story about how strongly our beliefs affect our physical bodies. He mentioned a football game that took place in Monterey Park, a Los Angeles suburb, where several people experienced the symptoms of food poisoning. The physician who examined interpreted that the cause was a certain soft drink from the dispensing machines, all of his patients had purchased prior to becoming ill. With this insight an announcement was made over the loudspeaker requesting people not to consume anything from the dispensing machine, describing how some people had become ill and the associated symptoms.

Immediately mayhem broke out in the stands as people vomited and fainted in multitudes. Some people who had not even been close to the machine fell ill. Ambulances from local hospitals that were overrun with calls as they had to travel back and forth carrying masses of plagued fans.

When it was discovered that the dispensing machine was not the culprit people instantly and "miraculously" recovered. We need to understand that our beliefs can make us sick or make us healthy in a jiffy. Beliefs have been known to affect our immune systems. And most importantly, beliefs can either give us the tenacity to take action or weaken and destroy our drive.

Schizophrenia Patients

Beliefs have the capacity to change both your mental and physical states. In a study on schizophrenia patients, scientists found that these individuals also possessed dual personalities and diverse belief systems. Therefore, the patient would not have diabetes when he existed as one of the personas but would have diabetes when he existed as the other personality. This illustrates how strong your beliefs can be and that they can instantly have a noticeable impact on your body.

Turning Your Values into a Mission

One of Mr. Jack Canfield's speeches featured a motivational story of "Tony Robbins," one of the most renowned gurus of peak performance and transformation. "Tony was in New York, and he wanted to feed the homeless people. He asked his staff to rent a van for themselves so that they could carry baskets of food for them. His staff came back saying "No vans available in the whole of New York, we can't do this today as all vans got booked for Thanksgiving." Tony did not take no for an answer and said common you are part of "Tony Robbins" anyone will help us with my name here, there are so many people with trucks, vans, and buses. Tony himself goes to stop one of the vans and introduces himself as Tony Robbins, explaining that he may have seen him on television and that he needed assistance with his van in order to feed the homeless. With a very buoyant look Tony thought he had got him convinced, but little did he know how mean people can be in New York. To his surprise, for the next 30 minutes, the entire team including Tony Robbins himself had no luck. Tony was offering them money and pleading but still, nobody was willing to help. That's something he learned about New York that day. People are not stopping or giving a hoot about what he's wanting to do. His whole team was like let's go have dinner and maybe do this some other time. But he just did not give up, he was persistent and mentioned that a victory was almost certain. It's just a game of numbers, he said. They eventually locate one man, who was the Captain of the Salvation Army. They couldn't have asked for a greater person to fulfill Tony's mission. It was a blessing! The captain then mentioned that he will suggest a better place that had burned down buildings and the people were really deprived of food and other assistance. On that day they helped a lot of lives.

So, when we want to make a difference in society, how far are we willing to go is a question we must ask ourselves. Being Tony Robbins he was willing to go from car to car looking for someone who could help. When you're on a mission it's all about how committed you are to your mission and how far you're willing to go to achieve it. One of Tony's core values has been serving people. We all have a lot to learn from this story of Tony Robbins",

All over the world, many people have given up things of their highest value for something that is not fulfilling. We need to discover our values and design our life as per our highest values. I learned from Arfeen Khan in one of his programs that our values are shaping our life and that every area of our life should be aligned to our values. That's when I first got my values listed down. I picked 6 values from a list of 200.

My highest values are in sequence:

1. Love

2. Making a difference

3. Gratitude

4. Spirituality

5. Youthfulness

6. Happiness

Your values may include integrity, family, passion, success, traveling, money, freedom, intelligence, connection, humanity, creativity, security, and so on.

Write down your top 6 values which form your baselines for living. I have designed my life around these 6 core values. This offers you a well-defined framework for the life you are creating, and these are the core values that you can prioritize the most.

If we don't go deep inside ourselves for what's meaningful and impactful in our lives, we will constantly be living someone else's idea of success and will never be able to find happiness and fulfilment. We will be happy and fulfilled if we are pursuing what is actually important and not becoming side-tracked by things like money, fame, or power that don't reflect our beliefs.

Our thoughts and our values are interlinked and based on the values; our life can be designed consciously.

Chapter 3

Exploring the Mind

If beliefs are the operating systems, then our minds will be the hardware as an analogy. It is really important to understand the nature of our minds. Once you understand how the mind works it becomes much easier to operate it as a tool. Just like when you buy a new device. It's best if we read the user's manual at the start rather than just trying to use it accidentally. We might end up learning accidentally, but we might not explore the different hacks and intricacies of it. The biggest reason why so many mental illnesses are happening around the world is just that we still haven't learned to use our minds in the best way possible. Most people are suffering from the intelligence of the mind. When I learned the different aspects of the mind from Sadhguru it made so much sense and gave me leverage in all aspects of life.

The mind has 16 parts, and they are categorized into 4 major parts that all humans possess. They are

1. Buddhi (The Intellect)

2. Ahankara (The sense of Identity)

3. Manas (The huge storage of Memory)

4. Chitta (Cosmic Intelligence)

Buddhi (The Intellect):

In the modern world intellect is being spoken as the mind however it is just 1 part of the mind. The intellect functions on the data accumulated and act as a data processor of conscious mind. People are often said to be intelligent when they seem to know more about a certain subject. That's their ability to store and retrieve that data efficiently. This is highly regarded in the modern world as the mind and the intelligence. However, this is just one aspect of the mind, and our mind has so many more aspects to it. The intellect has limited capabilities based on conscious data. Many times, you might have experienced that one might possess unconscious data, but they are not able to recollect and that's where the intellect would struggle to retrieve that data. The intellect is helpless in these cases as it is purely dependent on memory.

Ahankara (The sense of identity):

The intellect is a slave of the identity you have taken. The ahankara(identity) operates on different identities you associate yourself with. When you associate yourself with gender, race, religion, nation, club, and many more identities like them, your intelligence starts working for them. It is very important to set your identity consciously and to keep the identity limitless. The more identities you create your ability to access cosmic intelligence goes on reducing. One of the best ways to drop many identities that are typically associated with your body is to stop associating yourself with your body.

There is a practice in which you recite I'm not my body, Im not even my mind for 6-7 minutes every day with your awareness on your inhalation and exhalation. This practice if done daily can bring in awareness that you are more than just your body and mind. It allows you to drop the identities you carry associated with your body to a large extent.

Manas (The huge Silo of Memory):

Manas has many layers to it, and it is not only in the brain. It is all over the body. The intellect is only in your brain, but your entire body has memory and intelligence. This memory knows whether you are a man or a woman, the features of your ancestors, your skin tone, and so on. Every cell in the body has a memory of millions of years of generations. In ancient schools in India, the kids used to be taught to be identified with the universe and that's how the ability to access this vast amount of memory which is in our body is immensely enhanced. You may see when people can tap into more memory within themselves, they appear to be superhuman. It's best to keep our identity to limitless like the universe so that your intelligence works in tapping into the vast memory and intelligence in the entire cosmos.

Chitta (Cosmic Intelligence):

Chitta is a dimension of the mind which is not associated with memory. It is a dimension with endless possibilities. It is pure intelligence, the mind without memories. This intelligence is cosmic intelligence which is simply there all the time. This intelligence is always on whether you are awake or asleep. Chitta is the last point of the mind, and it connects to the basis of creation within you. It connects us with our consciousness. We would not be alive if our Chitta or intelligence within us was not on. Chitta is keeping us alive, keeping us going and making life happen. In yogic sciences, it's said that if we touch this dimension of the mind which is the linking point to one's consciousness, one doesn't have to even wish for anything, and the best possibilities just unfold.

Once we learn how to consciously keep our Chitta on, we don't need any assistance from anyone as the divine is working for us. Our perception and clarity will be crystal clear bringing the very core of our life close to us.

Nature of Thoughts

"Thought attracts that upon which it is directed." - Claude Bristol

Thoughts Create Our Reality:

The National Science Foundation published an article and stated that average humans have around 12000 - 60000 thoughts per day. Out of those 80% of the thoughts are negative and 95% of them are repetitive from the previous day. Our brain is relatively new in evolution and its main role is to make sure we are protected as a primal instinct. However, in the modern world, we don't have to worry about tigers attacking us, but that same hormone is being secreted constantly leading to stress, anxiety and depression. With overthinking negative aspects, your sympathetic nervous system is activated which puts your body on high alert. Our body loses its attention to the digestion system, reproductive system, and immune system, In these high alert states maintaining such states of fight and flight mode causes stress, anxiety, depression, weight gain, heart disease, and many other problems in our bodies. The cortisol was intended to keep us awake and alert so that we could survive. However here it's being used improperly now, which makes the body and the mind tired. Our negative thought patterns play the same thoughts over and over just like a set of playlists playing the same songs. So, if you have been trying to manifest financial abundance and 20% of your thoughts were positive and the rest 80% were negative then it is quite certain that you will be bound to attract debt and not abundance. The majority of individuals are never conscious of their thoughts, and they keep playing the same things time and again without realizing how it's impacting them. Only when you focus on those thoughts there are more projections of similar thoughts, and they just keep multiplying. Our mind only has the feature of addition and multiplication. Thus, if you can allow a negative thought pass by you, you're sparing yourself from its multiplication meaning if you give attention to that negative thought then more thoughts of a similar kind are produced. Now if you can be aware of your thoughts then you can very well prime your mind for the thoughts "You Want". Instead of focusing on things you don't want to manifest, you may train your mind to have ideas that are focused on the things you want. Being aware of your thoughts will help you control them and prevent you from paying attention to unfavourable ones. Not that you won't have negative thoughts, though. You just need to become aware of it and take control.

3 Factors that Influence the Quality of Your Thoughts:

1. Belief Systems

2. Past Experiences

3. Information

Belief Systems:

"Life is a competition" If this is a belief system then the thoughts would also in all spheres of life revolve around being competitive.

Past Experiences:

A person may cling to negative notions of trust if they have already experienced heartbreak from a lover in a relationship or a businessman being fooled. These beliefs are mostly unconscious. Even if those prior events may have occurred a long time ago, it's possible that they are still clinging to those beliefs because their reaction to those events was so strong that it had a lasting impact on their internal belief system at the time and is still active subconsciously now. They tend to generate thoughts that support the beliefs they hold.

Information:

There are numerous ways in which information from the news, the media, society, and your surroundings can programme your ideas. Consuming quality content is crucial.

Just the way you follow a diet for your food that is for your body. There is a diet required for your mind too. In today's age, there is a ton of harmful content everywhere that can influence your thoughts. Consuming healthy content is the need of the hour.

Here is a Method by which You can Control Negative Patterns of Thinking:

1. **Identify:** Whenever you have a negative thought you identify it and bring awareness to it.

2. **Break the pattern:** After bringing awareness you stop paying attention to that thought. This will break the pattern of continuously recurring negative thoughts.

3. **Switch:** You switch the negative thought to an empowering one.

Let me take a very common example where many people experience suffering. Consider a situation where you are recalling a person who said something to you, and you found it very offensive. Now you begin to chew in a manner similar to a cow that eats continuously throughout the day. When you keep thinking of an incident you keep reliving that moment and keep building negative emotions around it. When you relive the moment with your thoughts your subconscious mind doesn't know that it happened in the past. You are experiencing it in the present and sending those signals and chemicals to your entire body of what you felt during the experience. That's because those thoughts are creating a chemical reaction in your body and this chemical reaction is in these negative states. Ultimately, these thoughts are controlling your emotions and making you miserable. That's the reason you feel anger, pain, or hatred. This negative loop of thoughts and emotions ultimately starts taking a toll on your physical body as well as your energy has been affected and now you are vibrating at a very low frequency. If you continue to perform the negative loop you can get into mental trauma and other mental conditions related to depression, anxiety, and stress. To break this loop what you need to do is when u get that thought about that person or the incident you immediately forgive that person and stop thinking about that incident. Studies done by scientists show that when you are angry there are harmful chemicals that get secreted in your body. It's like you are producing poison in your body. Therefore, you can't expect the other person to suffer when you are consuming the poison. Being angry serves no purpose and hampers you in a negative way. When you let go and forgive that person you are out of bondage. Now, you replace it with a positive thought and acknowledge the good in that person. This not only liberates you from the bad feelings but also from cluttering your mind with negative thoughts. This exercise can help you combat negative thought patterns and channel your energy toward positive thoughts.

Manifestation Visualisation for Channelizing Thoughts and Emotions:

If it's about a love relationship, ask yourself what qualities you expect in your partner. Feel the emotions like you were actually with that person. Feel how he/she treats you and talks to you. Describe your ideal partner's appearance, including their skin, hair, smile, and other features. The greatest approach is to establish a thorough profile of your dream companion.

Define every aspect of what you want from your partner in your thoughts. Once you know exactly what you are looking for start visualizing yourself experiencing those moments in the present with real emotions. Hence, it is very important to first figure out exactly what you want and then have them in your thoughts and emotions. They are bound to manifest.

The Inspiring Story of Roger Bannister Breaking the World Record of a Mile within 4 Minutes.

For many years, experts claimed that it was impossible for a human to run a mile in under four minutes. The closest anyone may have achieved during that time was 4.01 in 1940. This was the pinnacle of achievement and the benchmark that could never be surpassed. People simply accepted it as a human limitation since they thought the experts were correct and that was the best humanly achievable.

Nobody ever broke the world record until 1954 when Roger Bannister successfully broke the 4 minutes record and recorded a timing of 3.59.4. What did he do to beat the world record that no one else could, then?

As part of Roger's practice, along with a focused and rigorous physical workout, he also included a mental workout in his practice. He used to visualize his outcome as if it were already true and he had already broken the record. He practiced this every day with strong emotions, visualization, and conviction. He programmed his mind and body to believe it is possible and created that certainty. Because of his certainty, the whole perception of the world changed towards the limitation aspect and in a year so many others broke the 4-minute mile record. He succeeded in breaking the illusion that it was impossible and inspired others to smash the record as well. Magic happens when you perform something with complete certainty, and it is scientific. I'm sure many of you have manifested something at some point. Although it might have happened by accident but there is a process to it. As a matter of fact, we possess the ability to use this to manifest whatever we want. Our brains have something known as RAS (Reticular Activating System). This identifies associations and determines which information should be focused on and which should be ignored. I'll give you an illustration: When you purchase a car, you immediately start to notice more vehicles that are similar on the roadways. It's not like there are more of those cars now. Your attention is just drawn to that car more since your brain has connected it to you. You simply weren't bothered to look at them earlier. So, your RAS is fully trained to give you the desired results when you have specific objectives, missions, or a vision and are focused on them with certainty. RAS programming is a magnificent technique that is used by many prosperous businessmen, athletes, and celebrities.

As much as your actions thoughts, emotions, and words are in harmony, you can set any record which nobody has ever achieved. It's essential to be mindful of what we focus on. We can have positive impacts if we keep our attention on the good things. In life we often limit ourselves with various thoughts like "Nobody has ever done it!", "It's impossible!", "I can't do it!", "I've tried everything!", and so on. Our mental conversations are among the most important factors that shape our reality. If you ask yourself, why am I so fat? Your mind is going to say, because you are a pig, right? Only when you ask empowering questions you will get empowering answers. If you ask yourself how do I lose 10 pounds? You will get a smart answer to this. You might answer it by saying I would start hitting the gym every day or increase my workout or follow a diet. The key is that you should communicate to yourself in a way that inspires you to come up with empowering solutions, for which you need to ask the right questions and focus on the right thoughts.

Start being aware of your thoughts, your visualizations, and your chatter with yourself. Are they empowering you or tearing you down?

Practising Samatva – Being Neutral

We often tend to label circumstances, situations, people, and things with good and bad. Creating likes and dislikes are the biggest reasons for one's misery. Liking something creates cravings and attachments while disliking something creates hatred and aversion. The Sankara part of the mind has the mental reactions of good and bad. While the Vinnana has the ability to witness and feel pure consciousness. We become conscious and are able to notice things as they are when we strengthen the power of our Vinnana and use it to the fullest extent. Overactive Sankara prevents us from seeing things as they actually are and causes us to constantly add new likes and dislikes. When we stop accepting things as they are and start expecting them to be a certain way for us, we keep losing our ability to accept them.

The powerful practice of avoiding labelling things as good or bad also sets you free from the notion of positive thinking. The idea of positive thinking first appears when something unpleasant comes to our mind.

You can develop the ability to concentrate on seeing things as they are when you don't categorise anything as positive or negative. This is referred to as Samatva in yoga. Samatva practise helps us engage our pleasure centres without any defined end goal or outcome, making it a tremendously potent instrument for life. As soon as your pleasure centres are awakened and unrestricted, you will begin to feel pure joy. To be happy, we don't really need a goal in mind. As soon as we accept reality, we are in the condition of Samatva. As a result, the next time an incident occurs, you should just observe it without giving it a label and instead concentrate your emotions and actions on finding a solution. Without using any terminology, concentrate on the solution.

Exercise:

1. Identify a situation you labeled bad

2. Ask if this could turn out to be the best thing that happened to you?

3. How do you make it the best thing that could possibly have happened to you?

For Eg:

1. **I was unable to clear the Microsoft job interview. I labelled it bad.**

2. **I learn to see it as the best thing that has ever happend to me. I would have to go through the trouble of relocating to a different city if I were to join there. I would need to find a new apartment and make new friends. So, it's actually a blessing that I'm not joining them.**

3. **I'll make sure that this interview rejection doesn't happen again when I apply to the next employer. I'll be very well-prepared**

and make sure not to make the same mistakes twice. I'm very glad Microsoft rejected me since it made me realize that I enjoy working for start-ups because there is immense learning and more career growth than in large corporations.

To move toward neutral, we want to use a scenario that is the positive opposite of what we want. It's as though you are at -50 and want to reach 0. Using a positive comparison, you try to shoot towards +50 to eventually get at 0. We want to maintain our labeling as impartial as we can.

Our tendency to label things as good or bad causes us to complicate our lives by being frustrated, stressed, or hurt when things don't go according to plan. In acknowledging it, we also release ourselves from the pain it causes.

Acceptance Makes Our Life Easier

Why does one individual not find something annoying while another finds it extremely annoying? Why is it that some people find it difficult to deal with a certain circumstance while others do so with ease? This is all due to the diverse interpretations each person gives to a specific event. They have assigned various interpretations to the same incident. There are many levels of perception.

It is important to accept things as they are to prevent these situations. In contrast, when you start associating things with meanings like love and hatred, good and bad, ugly and beautiful, you are creating strong connections that begin to appear. For example, "You say I hate this guy because he is too loud". This is perceived by your mind as loud=hate. Consequently, you have attached emotion to that action.

The feeling here is hatred. You develop a habit of hating his voice after experiencing it often to the point where it comes to you without being forced. Your brain will therefore send a signal to your body to start experiencing hate whenever that individual speaks. Then you begin to associate hatred with other obnoxious individuals. You fall prey to a circular pattern of action and response, action, and emotion in this way. It is an unpleasant emotion in this instance. Let's assume that you see him as he is. He may be noisy because he has been that way since he was young. You don't assign him any meanings or make any judgments about him because you accept him as he is. In this instance, you won't connect noisy people with hatred. You will be able to navigate life with the least amount of resistance because you will be able to see things as they are.

You enjoy viewing a rainbow because you accept it the way it is and don't speculate that it should be 500 meters to the left.

Secrets About Habits

According to yogic science, there is no such thing as good habits and bad habits. All habits are considered bad since you perform them unconsciously and mechanically. However, from a layman's perspective let's consider bad habits like overeating, smoking, alcohol, oversleeping, biting your nails, procrastination, and so on.

James Clear the Author of the best-selling book Atomic Habits states that there are 4 stages of any habit. These patterns are followed by the brain every time and in the same order.

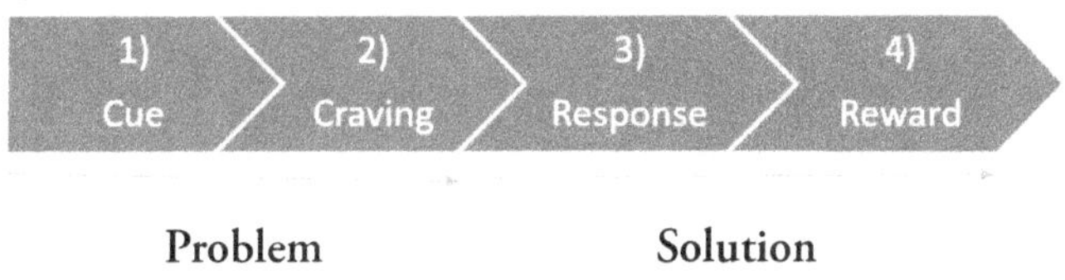

Problem   Solution

These 4 categories can be grouped as 1 & 2 being the problem phase while 3 & 4 being the solution phase.

Let's take a real-life example. You have an addiction to your phone, and you get distracted all the time.

1. **Cue: Your Phone beeps with some message tone.**

2. **Craving: You want to check your messages.**

3. **Response: You grab your phone and read the text.**

4. **Reward: You fulfill your craving by reading the texts. Grabbing your phone becomes associated with the phone buzzing.**

You can create new habits and break old habits with some frameworks.

How to Break a Bad Habit

1. Inversion of the 1st Law (Cue) - Make it Invisible.

There is a trigger for every behavior. Knowing the triggers, we should adjust our environment accordingly. If you smoke, make sure there are no ashtrays or cigarette crumbs in your immediate surroundings.

2. Inversion of the 2nd Law (Craving) - Make it Unattractive.

You should keep in mind the negative effects of smoking. Its shortcomings should stand out in your thoughts.

3. Inversion of the 3rd Law (Response) - Make it Difficult.

To overcome your bad behaviors, you must build barriers. You get rid of anything more than 100 percent, the more difficult it is to reach. Simply keeping cigarettes out of easy reach will help smokers cut back on their usage.

To avoid succumbing to peer pressure, avoid going to areas where you would smoke or smoke yourself. Peel an orange instead of lighting a cigarette. Change the response you usually have towards your craving.

4. Inversion of the 4th Law (Reward) - Make it Unsatisfying.

Have a companion who can hold you accountable for your actions. Publicize the severe consequences of your wrong behavior. Have a consequence for disobeying.

How to Create a Good Habit

The 1st Law (Cue) — Make it Obvious.

We can become aware of our behavior and patterns through awareness. When you become conscious, you can alter your brain's neural patterns.

For instance, if you want to get fit and healthy, arrange your environment such that you are surrounded by nutritious foods, inspiring images of people you admire, and motivational slogans. It should be clear that you are eager to form some positive new behaviors.

The 2nd Law (Craving) — Make it Attractive.

We need to make our habits attractive because it's the expectation of the reward that motivates us in the first place. Addicts to gambling experience dopamine when they place their bets rather than when they win.

More the anticipation more the dopamine levels and more are the chances for us to act. Try to highlight all the benefits of eating healthy food. Make it visually appealing and better to taste. Get your favorite fruits, vegetables and eateries that are healthy.

The 3rd Law (Response) — Make it Easy.

Take each day at a time. Don't be overwhelmed by the huge goal you have set and get demotivated thinking you are far from achieving your goal. It all starts small, and the only key is consistency and taking each day as it comes. Follow the process diligently and don't focus on the outcome. Following the process will inevitably get you to your goal.

Start working out for 2 minutes a day only. Do not think of the outcome, in the beginning, often we cancel our commitment to workouts because we think too far about it. If you focus on only wearing your gym gear, then the rest will automatically fall in place.

The 4th Law (Reward) – Make it Satisfying.

It is more common for us to repeat actions when they are very satisfying.

Take a luxurious shower with a high-end shower gel. After the workout, prepare your favorite fruit drink or a delicious breakfast for yourself. Do things that excite you and puts you in anticipation of the reward after the event.

For quitting any bad habits there are some simple strategies that you must apply that are highly effective:

1. Reason "Why"?

For any habit to be reprogrammed it needs strong emotions attached to a reason.

When you have a strong reason defined, it automatically creates a favorable situation for the mind to adapt and change. It's the emotions attached to the reason that play a big role. Ensure that the emotions are powerful. The stronger the habit the stronger are the emotions to be desired for that change.

If you do an exercise of answering these 3 questions alone, you will get clarity on your "why".

Ask yourself these questions:

1. What are the negative impacts of this habit?

2. If you correct this habit what are the best things that will happen?

3. What emotions do you feel seeing the future self without those habits?

This exercise will help you get the reasons and emotions out in the open.

2. Becoming Conscious and Reprogram your mind and body

Your brain stores every action or memory in the form of neurons. Therefore, the neurons form a communication thread when you are executing a certain activity. The connection keeps getting stronger and the task becomes easier to complete more the times that action is performed. For instance, learning to drive or ride a bike takes some practice. But with enough repetition, the brain forges these neural connections, and the memory is hardwired. Because they were practiced frequently, harmful behaviors are wired in this way.

Bring awareness to the below aspects to make changes:

What triggers your bad habits to start?

How many times in a day do you do it?

When does it happen?

Who is around you?

Where are you?

Scientists have recently proven that it just takes 30 days of daily repetition without missing a day for your brain to get wired with anything. If you can make the repetition process last longer, you can finish it sooner.

Because neuroplasticity is something that is possible until death, you can consciously reprogram your brain. However, it becomes far more difficult to rewire your brain as you age. As a result, you'll discover that changing elderly individuals is difficult.

Your brain begins to develop patterns when you are living subconsciously, and these patterns begin to take place automatically. Consider yourself as the remote control, and the TV the body and mind. You should have the freedom to choose the station you want to watch, and you should have the option to switch channels whenever you want. Nevertheless, if the channels begin to operate and change on their own, you lose control. That is what most people experience. The unconscious patterns have taken control of their mind and body. People have fallen prey to the mind's unconscious thinking habits that are controlling them. Your body and mind should be under your complete control, and they should obey all your commands. But when you live unconsciously, it's like how a TV works without a remote control thanks to repeated patterns of the past. When a pattern is recognised, it can be deliberately broken and replaced with an empowering association or action.

You're intended to break the association in the brain and alter the pattern. If smoking makes you feel good, try associating it with pain instead. If you enjoy sleeping excessively, then associate sleeping with laziness instead of pleasure. Any habit is simply a compulsive mental behaviour that runs through your subconscious, but you have the power to become conscious of it and alter the pattern with practise.

Repeat this procedure over and over until the new pattern has become deeply engrained. Usually, a month's worth of repetitions or an equivalent number of regular practises are needed.

3. Reward

Give yourself a reward each time you replace an old habit with a new one. The brain receives a signal that this new task offers advantages, and it will begin to accept the new activity. With the money you've been saving on your liquor purchases every time, you could get a great piece of clothing for yourself. Anything that makes you happy and fulfilled is something you should do. Keep providing the brain with the rewards it requires.

4. Having the Right Influence

The biggest influence on our behavior, attitude, and outcomes comes from the individuals we surround ourselves with. If you want to change the way your body and physical health look and you hang out every day with a group of uninspired, unfit, and careless individuals, then it is quite likely that you will be modeling your lifestyle like them. In contrast, spending time with reliable, committed, and physically fit people who are better than you in sports or fitness will inspire you to succeed. Have a group of friends, communities, or mastermind groups who share your interests.

5. Environment

If you want to stay in shape, fill your kitchen with wholesome foods instead of junk food that will tempt you to make poor choices. According to the study, eating chocolate regularly by someone with sugar cravings is lowered by 70% when the chocolate is kept in a difficult-to-reach location and requires the use of a chair. When implemented in our daily lives, such straightforward techniques can assist us in breaking undesirable behaviors. Additionally, you can hang up images of motivational posters for good health to affect your subconscious. On a vision board that you can view every day, post a picture of your ideal self. Our actions and behaviours are significantly influenced by our environment.

Overcoming Stress

What really causes you Stress?

If I ask you what is causing your stress, you might give me a long list that includes things like your finances, health, job, and other things. However, there is only one thing that is making you anxious. You're not getting the results you want. You have expectations for everything and want things a certain way. You refuse to consider all possible outcomes. The result might not always go your way.

How do you overcome this Stress?

1. **Acknowledge** - This is what happened. Although it is not how I had hoped, it did happen.

2. **Actions:** Pay attention to the steps you will take. Focus on the process rather than the outcome.

Why do humans experience stress? People frequently link stress and pressure in a direct way. Unfortunately, it is not how stress is perceived. Stress includes both the strain and your resilience to deal with it.

Stress = Pressure ÷ Resilience

Depending on how well each person can handle pressure, various people may react differently to the same situation. People frequently link stress and pressure in a direct way. Stress and pressure are directly related, however resilience as the common denominator is rarely considered. There will always be pressure since stress cannot exist without pressure. However, the factor that affects stress the most is resilience.

The capacity to bounce back swiftly from adversities is called resilience. It is possible to create resilience within yourself. Extreme resilience enables you to manage any circumstance calmly and doesn't even depress you. Depending on their level of resilience, different people respond differently to various situations. When someone master's resilience, they just don't fall down no matter what life throws at them. We will experience all types of setbacks in life at various levels in every aspect of our lives. You are frequently mentally and emotionally broken by these setbacks. It causes us to hibernate or slide downward. You may train yourself to become unaffected by any circumstances in life if you have resilience.

Keanu Reeves, a well-known actor best recognized for his work in "The Matrix," has an inspirational life story and is regarded as one of the most resilient public figures in the world. From the point where they enter the profession until the point where they become very successful, the lives of celebrities are difficult. In Keanu's case, his personal life was also in a great deal of turmoil. Keanu's father abandoned him when he was just two or three years old, and then his mother did the same.

Considering his dyslexia, he had difficulty adjusting to school. His high school alone required him to switch between 5 different institutions. His mother had three quick remarriages before settling in Canada, making him the son of three stepfathers. Despite having such a tough upbringing, his dedication and passion for acting eventually brought him to Hollywood, where he soon experienced tragedy as well. Shortly after his best friend, an actor who worked with him passed away, his sister who was close to him, was diagnosed with Leukemia. Besides his monotonous life as an actor, this was another severe blow to him. He later met Jennifer the love of his life, with whom he was about to have a child when she suffered from stillbirth. Jennifer also died in a car accident not long after their baby died. This was a huge setback for him. All of these occurrences in a celebrity's life might cause intense feelings of melancholy in anyone. He kept a low profile for a while as he dealt with his sadness. Additionally, he made an effort to revive his career by bringing 47 Ronin, which was a miserable failure. Everyone assumed he would be done acting and would never return.

However, his perseverance prompted him to participate in the creation of "John Wick," a huge global blockbuster franchise. Keanu Reeves is one of today's most recognizable performers due to his kindness and charity. He owns his own foundation for charity and makes significant donations to charitable trusts. Without his perseverance, we would never have met a beautiful person like Keanu, who has been giving thousands of people a hand up through his foundation. One needs a strong mindset to bear so much strain when dealing with millions of admirers, demanding schedules, endless projects, media interviews, and so much more.

Here is a useful activity for boosting resilience that I learned in Sri Kumar Rao's book The Personal Mastery Program.

You are the civil engineer of your life, laying the foundation for a prosperous, fulfilling, and pleasant existence. If a mountain, swamp, and forest were present, you would have to construct a bridge. It wouldn't make you angry. The hurdles, adversities, and toxic people who enter your life are what make up the forest, mountain, and swamp. Even after facing numerous difficulties, you don't lose patience with them; instead, you work through them and decide how to forge ahead with your plans for the future. With this perspective towards our challenges , it can make us exponentially resilient in life.

Hardships and Challenges are a Boon

A man once discovered a butterfly's cocoon. A little gap became visible. He sat and watched the butterfly try to fit its body through that tiny hole for several hours. Up until that point, when it appeared to have reached a dead end. So, the man made the choice to assist the butterfly. He grabbed a pair of scissors and cut the last portion of the cocoon off. The butterfly then easily emerged but having a bloated body and tiny, shrivelled wings.

The man didn't give it much thought and waited for the butterfly to be supported by the shrivelled wings as it lay there. But it didn't go like that. The rest of the butterfly's life was spent crawling around with little wings and an enlarged body since it was unable to fly.

Despite the man's good intentions, he was unaware that God made the butterfly's struggle to fit through the narrow opening and the tight cocoon to press fluid from the butterfly's body on its wings so that they would be prepared for a flight when it emerged from the cocoon.

Moral of the Story:

The challenges we face in life enable us to develop our capabilities. Without challenges, we never learn and never become stronger, thus its crucial for us to tackle the problems and learn from experiences rather than constantly complaining about them. Embrace difficulties and challenges with positivity.

We only learn to deal with issues when they are constantly presented to us throughout life. You continue to get wiser and stronger as you solve problems. The most important life lessons are frequently learned via failure.

Clifford Young ran an incredible 875 km to achieve a world record in the shortest amount of time.

One of the hardest races to even accomplish was an 875 km marathon in Australia that ran from Sydney to Melbourne. It demanded intense levels of preparation, physical fitness, mental vitality, and endurance.

A 61-year-old farmer appeared to have joined the race. He appeared extremely out of place wearing non-athletic clothing and work boots. He was asked if he was at the right place and if he was thinking of running this. He said that he owns a flock of sheep that he occasionally runs for days.

In addition to the fact that this race was a wonderful fit for his schedule, he noted that he runs with them to stay in shape. He simply wanted to compete in a race of this kind and understood nothing whatsoever about it. He didn't even understand the rules or the training needed for it. As a result, when the race started, all the other competitors—who were all young people—sprinted and had a significant lead, whereas Clifford ran slowly and at his own speed. Clifford was unaware that the other runners typically ran for approximately 18 hours and slept for about 6 hours. He thought that this was a race that went on around the clock.

He just kept running because no one was there to tell him his limits or to stop him. Eventually, he finished the race two days earlier than usual and in a record-breaking 5 days, 15 hours, and 4 minutes. This is a classic example of overcoming obstacles, being resilient, and not holding yourself back. Someone who was accustomed to overcoming obstacles when working with cattle in the wild was also capable of accomplishing a race. The game's rules were completely unknown to him. He believed they had to run nonstop for the entire day. He was completely unaware that the other players slept for six hours every day.

He continued to run as the other players slept. He disproved the myth that professional marathon runners cannot go without sleeping because he is a beginner. The other professional athletes were all prevented from pursuing this opportunity by restricting their beliefs.

Numerous professional sportsmen have now adopted Cliff's strategies and have started round-the-clock running as a result of his victory.

We frequently end up adopting beliefs about what is possible and what is not. The truth is that you must hold yourself to the highest standards with your beliefs and attitudes, though. Clifford had an optimistic outlook and no limiting beliefs, which enabled him to accomplish the impossible.

The "One Thing" in Personal Growth

We are all aware that new activities are required to produce new results. Everyone wants extraordinary results, but we cannot expect extraordinary results from regular acts. Therefore, we must adapt our activities and behaviors accordingly. Most people wish to alter their activities and behaviours, yet they are constrained by emotional triggers. Procrastination, rage, fear, reflection, envy, stress, sloth, low self-esteem, lack of confidence, and other emotional states are examples of these. You will most certainly not achieve your goals in these states. We must be in peak states to perform at our best. Therefore, we must learn the technique of being at peak states if we want to be able to master life.

What is the most crucial instrument that would be determining the quality of our lives, asked one of the reporters to Tony Robbins, one of the most well-known instructors in personal growth.

Our decision regarding the beliefs, emotions, and thinking will be influenced by your state. The "State" you are in, according to him, is the one factor that controls all your results. Those who are experts in controlling their state can achieve great things in life! The most important skill that will determine destiny is the ability to be able to consciously create the state you desire.

Now imagine what would happen if we had complete control over our thought and emotions. We might be anywhere at any time. We are endowed with this superpower. However, many of us have fallen prey to the mind's unconscious thinking habits. We are capable of intentionally determining our state. No outside forces would ever endanger our state if we could begin consciously determining it. Anytime we feel like it, we can be in a loving, joyous, appreciative, or inspired condition.

"Your boss fired you"

"You lost a million-dollar deal"

"You lost a dear one"

"Your partner doesn't love you like before"

"You had an accident"

"Your kids don't listen to you"

You might still be in states of gratitude, inspiration, compassion, joy, serenity, youthfulness, optimism, hope, happiness, admiration, and pride even if you went through any of the above circumstances. These conditions won't bring you down.

These are positive emotional states that will enable you to vibrate more strongly. You can consciously decide to be in these states. Every one of us has the capacity to be in any state we choose. When we make the decision to be in a positive vibration, we begin attracting those situations into our lives as well. The way we feel affects the way we think, and the way we think affects the way we feel. Therefore, it's crucial to take control of our thoughts and feelings and not let them be influenced by anything outside of us. We can be joyful whenever we want once we are able to separate ourselves from everything outside that influences our thoughts and emotions.

Chapter 4

Mastering Our Emotions

How we feel within is a choice we hold. If we are wondering, why are we sad instead of happy is just because of the absence of our awareness. We always hold the choice of our state of mind. What we practice gets stronger. When we practice being sad all the time the mind gets accustomed to those patterns and the body with the chemicals that release along with it. Over time we get addicted to those chemicals and patterns and unconsciously our body and mind create situations to experience sadness.

How we feel within is something that happens due to these patterns of emotions and will take us into automatic states if we are not consciously crafting it. Compulsive behaviors in our physiology, language, and habits will keep happening.

There are 3 important things that control how you feel.

1. Physiology

Simply said, physiology is the way you use your body. The Wonder Woman and Superman positions, where your hands are on your hips and your body is erect, were identified in a study on power poses by Harvard University as postures that enhance testosterone levels by 30%, reduce cortisol levels by 35%, and increase action likelihood by 33%. These stances obviously give you greater assurance and encourage you to act to get better results.

Therefore, you can significantly alter your results only by adjusting your body language. Along with the posture,

Your breathing

Your tone

Your volume

Your body language

Your physiology can be altered by physical activities or exercises.

A depressed man would have tiny, shallow breaths, a low, squeaky voice, antagonistic body language, and all these characteristics. It is possible for anyone to say this. As a result, your body reflects the situation you are in, and you may change your physiology to alter your state. Most people unintentionally adopt physiological postures that they have become habituated to and conditioned to. They enter those states connected to that physiology automatically as a result. For some stages, the physiology is essentially the same in various people. By being aware of your physiology, these states can be quickly changed from a negative to a positive one.

According to yoga, how you breathe determines how you feel. When we are furious, pleased, sad, or depressed, we breathe differently. Therefore, regardless of the state you have been in, you can alter your state of mind if you just change your breathing and practise deep conscious breathing for two minutes. Our physiology and our thoughts are controlled by our breath. Similar to this, you can alter different components of your physiology to alter your state.

2. The Pattern of Language

Words are like seeds. If you continue to say certain things, you are giving life to them. The words you use have the power to either bless or curse your life. Our mental state is frequently expressed in the language we use to communicate with ourselves and others. We often don't realise of how much unconscious self-deprecating language we possess. You may not be aware how habituated you are to some sentences which are limiting, and you frequently repeat them. Perhaps you say it out of irritation, rage, or obsessive behaviour, or maybe you view it as a joke.

Words have meanings and meanings lead us to experience certain emotions and we often vibrate in a certain way when we feel a certain emotion. Different words have different energies and vibrations.

Language is quite interesting and there is magic in the way we speak and use it. Most people use toxic language toward themselves without realising how it affects their subconscious and governs their lives.

There are certain words that will magnify human emotion while there are certain words that will lower human emotions. Let's consider the example of your favourite speaker

They have the power to affect you emotionally and move you. This is so that they can emotionally connect with others through the magic of words. Now, the language you use and the words you choose when you speak to yourself influence the mindset you are in. Speaking empowering words can put you in a high-energy, positive frame of mind, while speaking harmful words will put you in a negative, low frame of mind.

Start being conscious of your inner dialogue as well as the words you choose to use. Therefore, the majority of what you believe is based on incantations. You repeat it over and over while feeling strongly emotional about it. As a result, unlike affirmations, your entire neurological system receives those signals and recognizes that you genuinely mean what you say, unlike affirmations.

Affirmations are a little different from incantations. Affirmations can be said without emotional intensity. Let me give you an example of the power of unconscious incantation which is a true incident. Every day I used to park my car under my apartment at an angle where my car windshield will be right under the building's apartments. My dad used to say your windshield will break don't park it there. Anyone could drop something and can break your windshield. He kept saying your windshield glass will break again and again with so much intensity every time I would visit my parents. You won't believe to my surprise in 20 days the unexpected happened. I was on a business trip to Mumbai, and I had parked my car outside my hotel, I walk across to my car and see a big crack on my car's windshield. Not sure how and who did it. But it surely did not happen the way my dad was expecting. It broke at an outdoor street parking in a different city outside a hotel. That is the power of incantation, he used to say it almost every day with so much emotional intensity that your windshield will break as if it had already happened. Finally, it did manifest. I wondered anything else from my car could have broken, why the windshield? The breaking of the windshield is such a rare phenomenon and has never happened in my life. Yet that unusual incident happened soon after his incantations.

If you notice in your life, you will find so many instances where reality has been shaped by incantations. Most people incant unconsciously. These incantations look like

"The market is so bad"

"So many people are falling sick"

"It is so difficult"

"I'm so stressed"

"I'm not good at this"

"I can't do without my phone"

"Life is hard"

"I can't do this"

"I've become so fat"

When these kinds of words are spoken, your energy levels drop right away, your inner emotions change, and your vibration also alters. You may change the energy simply by using words. Words have the ability to drastically alter your life. So, by frequently using these kinds of statements, you make it a reality for yourself. By using a positive vocabulary for yourself, you can even alter your surroundings.

When you say, "I'm so stressed," you are essentially basing your statement on some past occurrences to which you have assigned a stress-related meaning. Your interpretation of these occurrences is crucial in this situation. These situations might be stressful to one individual while inspiring, enjoyable, or challenging to another. You may say "Things are challenging" or "I'm learning" or "I'm growing" instead of "I'm so stressed." You see what I mean. Don't give events bad meanings because doing so will only lead to bad results.

This is something I have seen in a lot of folks. The hospitality sector was among the first industries to be impacted when the pandemic struck. The phrase "The market is too terrible" used to be repeated by one of my close pals. This remark would carry strong emotions with it in every conversation, almost to an extreme. This would continue with friends and family for months. Guess what, he started shaping his world. He began to receive poor deals.

His business associates and clientele started taking advantage of him. He began to receive consumers who paid little. Even though many businesses had recovered and were doing absolutely fine, in his industry as a whole. However, he was preoccupied with the drawbacks and had them ingrained in his mind. He overlooked the opportunities and concentrated solely on the problems. He could have focused on potential fixes and solutions. He kept chanting that the market was poor all the time, and finally he began to draw a decline in his business.

I was coaching him at that time, and I made him aware of his behaviour while insisting that he quit incanting them. I advised him to change such phrases to the ones that were empowering and to embrace gratitude every day. Good opportunities began to present themselves to him within the same week, and for the first time in months, all his service apartments were fully booked. He noticed quick benefits.

The languages we speak often control our attitude, behavior, mindset and perception towards life. A study was done by a popular behavioral economist Keith Chen where he was comparing the thinking patterns of people who spoke "Futureless" and "Futured" languages. Futured languages like English distinguish between the past, present and future. Whereas languages like Chinese use same phrases for past, present and future.This study revealed that people who spoke Chinese were 30% more likely to save money annually for the future and since people who speak English make the future quite distant from the present making them less motivated to save for the future.

Often people create identities with the language patterns they use. Once you create an identity the intellect of the mind will work on protecting it. This identity they create consciously or unconsciously could work both ways, with some people it works in their favor while it works as a curse for the latter. People who create identities are more likely to have noticeable results in line with the identity they create.

Statistics shows that:

People who call themselves lucky are more lucky than others.

This is because they see better opportunities, make better decisions and have a positive outlook towards life. This mindset and belief makes them lucky.

People who call themselves "a foodie" are more likely to be fat.

People who consider themselves organized are more likely to do everything in an organized manner.

People who call themselves a voter are more likely to vote than someone who just considers voting as an activity.

We should be extremely careful on the identities we create for ourselves with the language we use. Our identities shape our thoughts, actions and behaviors.

3. Focus

"You Do not Feel an Emotion You Do an Emotion."

You have an unbelievable gift of being aware and changing your state whenever you want. Being a hero is nothing but merely a state of mind. At any given point you hold the power to consciously change your state.

Let's do a simple exercise. Close your eyes and try out this exercise

- "Think of a moment you have been really proud of yourself." Feel those emotions. Live and experience that moment for a minute.

- Now think of something you can be grateful for.

- Think of something that is extremely exciting for you.

In each of these tasks what you did was simply focused and brought your attention to each of these emotions. You were able to enter empowering and positive states of admiration, thankfulness, and joy solely by bringing your attention to the situation.

You can similarly tune into love, inspiration, kindness, and so many other positive states. The problem why most people get stuck in low vibrational states is because they focus on the bad things which could lead to negative outcomes. This inevitably takes them to those same states of pain, anger, resentment, jealousy, anxiety, fear, etc leading to negative outcomes. When that happens, the unconscious programs keep repeating and the mind takes over the body.

If you focus on events of anxiety, you will have more anxiety. If you focus on events of pain, you will have more pain.

For instance, when a person smokes, their body becomes so habituated to the pattern that the brain is aware of when and under what circumstances it would be necessary to smoke. For instance, if you just finished eating your meal and have the habit of smoking afterward, your brain will signal you to start smoking right away.

These are unconscious patterns, and the body has become accustomed to them. When this rhythm is broken, the body feels extremely uncomfortable. As soon as you start to make a change you will hear a voice inside of you saying "Oh common, you are stressed out. You can relax a bit and smoke a cigarette. There is nothing wrong with only 1 cigarette. Even your coworkers smoke cigarettes.

Do you relate to these voices inside you when you attempt to change?

- "Common, you can start working out from Monday"

- "Just one drink"

- "Oh common, you can have a cheat day today with that Pizza. You have had such a stressful week."

- "You can go back to sleep; you don't have to wake up at 6 am on a Sunday."

Your mind and body will push you toward your comfort zone. It will push you towards familiarity. Real growth happens when you can overcome these patterns of the mind. This pattern can only be broken with complete awareness.

Golf Champion Visualization

The inspiring story of Jack Nicklaus who is a world champion in Golf. Before taking a shot, he would always visualize the ball being hit so brilliantly that it went inside, and he is celebrating. To execute the best shot with his subconscious mind, he harnessed the strength of his imagination with his conscious mind. He chose to focus on the positive and visualize optimistic outcomes.

How to Break Mental and Emotional Patterns

Patterns can be Broken by 3 Steps

Identify – Identify the pattern of negative thought or emotion.

Stop – Stop giving attention to that thought or emotion and do not focus on it. Energy flows where attention goes!

Replace – Now replace that negative thought or emotion with an empowering one.

Curing Lukemia

David Seidler a popular Screenwriter for the movie Kings Speech was also a stutterer like King Geroge VI in the movie. He cured cancer using the power of visualization and became cancer-free for over a decade now. In an interview with CNN, he mentioned that he would spend hours everyday visualizing and when he went for surgery after days, the doctor with a startled look mentioned that he doesn't see cancer anymore. The doctor was so amazed and found it hard to believe. He sent the scans to 4 other centers just so that he could confirm it right.

David used to do a form of visualization meditation wherein every day he would visualize his nice cream-colored unblemished bladder lining. He would do it every day and visualize his cancer being cured. With the power of visualization and repetition, he cured himself by programming his subconscious. When certain programs are given to your mind, your mind works on a cellular level. It's like the mind is the CEO and the trillions of cells you possess are the employees. The CEO is giving the commands. So, it's all about whether you are a good CEO giving the right commands of happiness, love, and gratitude to your body or a bad CEO giving commands of anxiety, stress, and depression. Your cells react based on the commands given by the mind. Choosing to focus on your well-being rather than on self-deprecating thoughts and emotions is the key. You need to remember that what you practice becomes stronger.

How to overcome being upset?

One of the major reasons for people to have negative emotional states is because they are upset about someone or something. To overcome these situations, you need to ask yourself a couple of questions to understand why you feel a certain way.

1. What is the belief I have about that person, thing, or situation that is upsetting me?

2. When I held this belief, what is the impact on me? How do I feel?

3. Who would I be without this belief? – Will I be relaxed? Would I be closer to that person/ thing/situation? Do I need to be less pushy? Do I need to be more accepting? Do I need to be less

judgemental? I need to release my beliefs to accept that person/thing/situation the way it is.

4. Now think of 3 good traits, qualities, or reasons to be grateful for that person/thing/situation. No matter how bad you think it was, you must be willing to accept, let go and see the best.

Practices for Mental, Emotional and Spiritual Well Being

1. Pranayama

Prana means life energy and Yama means to control. There have been various scientific studies done and numerous research papers have been published on how our breath is related to our mental, emotional, and physical well-being and enhances our ability to experience life.

Our breath is directly related to our mind and body. If our breath changes our body and mind also get affected. And if our mind or body is in a certain state it affects the way we breathe.

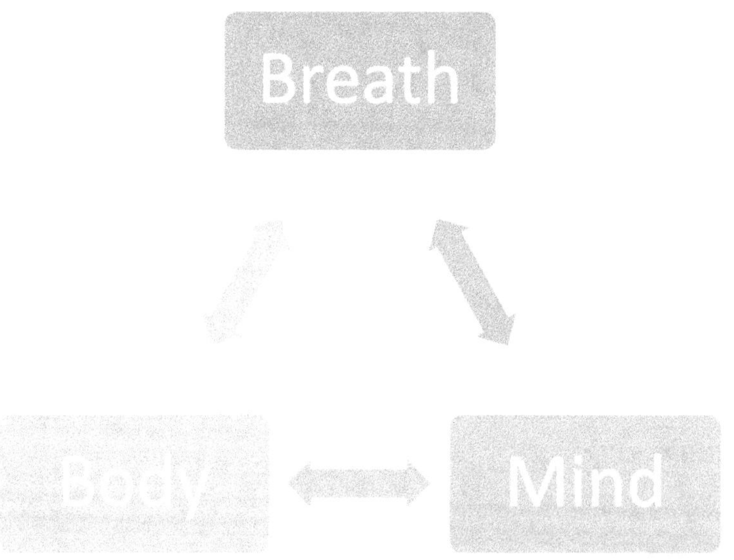

Prana is that vital energy in our body, which we call life energy.

Your emotions are directly influenced by your breathing. So various emotions can be affected by breath. Slow breathing activates the vagus nerve which essentially calms the body, slows down the heart rate, and decreases blood pressure.

The respiratory rhythm also controls some of the activity in the brain regions involved in attention, wakefulness, and anxiety. How we breathe can directly influence the brain.

United States Navy medical team is using this technique for their Navy SEALS to remain calm and composed in dangerous combat situations.

Breathing Exercise:

It is a 4-step process in one cycle.

Step 1: Exhale for 4 counts

Step 2: Hold for 4 counts

Step 3: Inhale for 4 counts

Step 4: Hold for 4 counts

You can repeat this cycle at your convenience for 5 minutes and then gradually start increasing as per your time and appetite. Similarly, there are various Pranayama techniques that help align your life energies and work on your emotions, body and mind. Some of the most popular ones are Bhramari, Bhastrika, Anulom Vilom, SuryaBhedan, Chandrabhedan and Ujjayi.

So, if there is a level of mastery on your Pranayama and you take charge of your life energies, then it is 100% guaranteed that you will never have any psychological ailments. Your physiological system will be taken care of up to 90% as it depends on other factors like weather, pollution, food, and other influencing elements. However, 90% is still quite good and can keep you in great shape for most of your life. Pranayama is such a powerful breathing practice that helps you take charge of the vital forces of your very existence. It is best to do it for a duration of 20 minutes as the chemicals in the body start to secrete in good quantities when you do it for that amount of time. Our human system is the most sophisticated machine on this planet and its high time we start learning how it operates at its best.

2. Mind Cleaning Exercise

For 10 minutes every day in the evenings or at night visualize all the impressions accumulated over the day dissipating like smoke from the rear of your tailbone to the back of your forehead. This helps you cleanse your mind and makes you feel much lighter. Just the way you brush your teeth every day, if you understand the importance of cleaning your mind, you will see a significant change in your life. Imagine you drop some curry on your favourite dress, just the way you might do something immediately to remove the stain rather than those stains becoming for a lifetime. The very same thing happens with the mind. We often end up leaving horrible stains in our minds which were never addressed or cleaned. We hold on to what people said or did many years back. Rather we clean it out of our minds the very same day for our own mental and emotional well-being. Suppressing those thoughts and emotions can have negative effects. Hence cleaning them is the ideal way to deal with them.

3. Anapana Sati Meditation by Gautam Buddha

Ana means inhalation and Pana means exhalation and Sati means awareness. In this simple meditation, all you are doing is being aware of your breath i.e inhalation and exhalation. As a result, you must be fully conscious of both your inhalation and exhalation when you breathe in and out, respectively. If any thought arises ignore it and return your attention to your breath. This technique automatically reduces the thoughts you have. You may reduce any thoughts and begin connecting with the life force within you if you do it with complete awareness. This is a very powerful technique to sharpen the mind.

4. Living in the Moment

Most people experience anxiety, stress, and sadness as a result of their own memories, feelings, and thoughts. People are affected by their pasts and worried about their futures. Individuals are suffering from both what happened two years ago and what might happen two days from now.

I was a victim of a syndrome to an extent where I used to live only in the past or the future neglecting the present. Above all, I would think of all undesirable events that might occur in the future. So, I was turning my own intelligence against myself. I didn't understand the significance of living in the moment or how much of our reality we create until I started engaging in spiritual practises. Therefore, if we can come to terms with the fact that all we have is this moment, that's when we can start using our intelligence more effectively for our own good.

With negative thoughts, we tend to drain a lot of our energy. An interesting study done by Cornel University stated that 85% of what generally people keep worrying about never happens and with the 15% of the time that anything negative happens, 79% generally handled it better than expected. Therefore, it is completely pointless to waste our energy on negative thoughts that we are creating in our own minds. Our creative conscious mind must be used to achieve beneficial results. So, can we actively pursue happiness by beginning to appreciate this moment? Can we begin to live in the present moment knowing that this is all we have? We are unable to travel into the future or the past.

Furthermore, the suffering we experience is ultimately only an illusion or past projections. The mind tends to get into compulsive behaviour and one of the best ways to get out of these states is to centre yourself in the present and be conscious. It is quite easy to get out of a compulsive state by just bringing awareness to your breath. This technique will help you stop giving attention to your compulsive thoughts. Focus on your breath and you will see you can quickly come back to the present. Since the time I learned this, I have been trying to create my present consciously. All that exists is, this moment, and you have the power to feel the way you want. You create the emotions of this moment. So, if you wish to focus then you can choose to be happy! Choose to be grateful! Choose to be inspired!

If the key to your state of mind is within you, would you choose to be angry or joyful?

Obviously, you would want to be joyful. However, it is the compulsive program of the mind that puts you in that angry frame.

Because you've practiced being angry a lot over the years and your mind has given significance to many different things that make you upset. Therefore, your subconscious is operating on autopilot for you. Any time one of these incidents occurs, you get angry right away. However, if you know that you want to be happy and that being angry can lead to sadness, anxiety, and high blood pressure, you probably don't want to be in this mood. So, it's only when you are conscious, that you choose what state of mind you wish to be in. So, if we have the ability to choose to be in the desired state at any given time, no outside force can have an impact on us. We must practice being pleased, just as we have practiced being angry.

Exercise:

There is a wonderful exercise I learned from BK Shivani. It involves stopping for one minute each hour to think about your thoughts, gaining awareness of your thoughts and rerouting them to the thoughts you desire. If we can control our thoughts, we can alter the course of our lives with just a few one-minute intervals for thought observation. In my opinion, it's better to direct comedies and upbeat films in our mind than horror ones.

Chapter 5

The Magic Sauce – Strategies for the Modern World

We all want to have a wonderful life but not everyone does, because everyone applies different standards, beliefs, strategies, and coping mechanisms to their life. If you look, most people in the world who have managed to achieve huge accomplishments are those who have been successful in making significant contributions have worked on certain fundamental elements that have moulded their lives into what they are today.

And I've listed some characteristics that were shared by all these people below.

The 4 Most Important things that must be changed to live a life of fulfilment, happiness and peak performance that leads to growth in every area of your life are:

1. Setting High Standards

2. Changing Your Limiting beliefs

3. Having a Game Plan

4. Having Good Relationships

1. Setting High Standards

Someone who has a chaotic life and yet is not doing anything about it is because they have set very low standards. They might still be quite content with it as they would have low aspirations and somewhat snuggled up in their comfort zone.

85

Have a desire for more from yourself in every area of your life. It's good to have desires, however you should make them consciously.

Examples:

I will wake up at 6 am every day no matter what.

I must have "X" amount of money by "Y" year.

I will be at X position by this year.

I will have meaningful and lasting relationships with friends, family, work and peers.

I will spend quality time with my Lover/Family/Child/Friend

My weight will be "X" by "Y" year

I will practice 5 mins of meditation every day for my mental well-being.

I will practice consciously being happy each day.

These are some of the examples of setting standards in every area of your life and each of these points can be written down in detail

You must set a bar for yourself and stick to it. It has to be a must and not a should. Use it in all areas of your life as shown in the diagram below. You must leave your comfort zone. Have a mechanism of penalty for yourself if you don't uphold your standards. Have an accountability partner or a coach who is continually pushing you if you are unable to complete the task on your own. Our thoughts, words, actions, and behaviors should be in line with the standards we are setting. Achieving our milestones won't be possible if we have set a high standard, but our thoughts are still of a low frequency. We set high goals for ourselves in order to be in the best possible shape, but if we don't take significant steps to live up to those standards, the desired result won't be achieved. Some of the greatest individuals on this planet set really high standards and alter their beliefs, thoughts, words, actions, emotions, behaviours and values to actually change their destiny.

Tony Robbins who is currently regarded as one of the world's most accomplished success coaches, once set high standards in every area of his life, as shown in the figure below. He started everything from scratch and is the epitome of being a hero from zero.

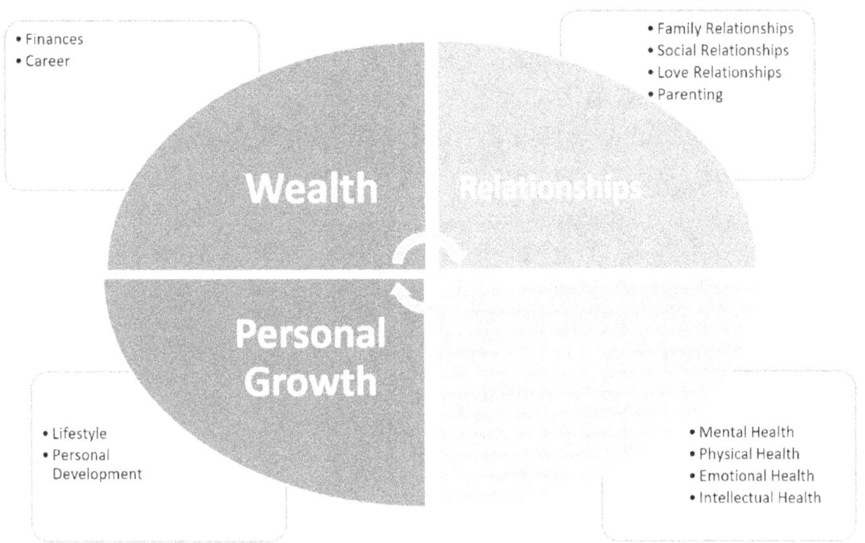

Mr. Robbins has coached several notable figures including Nelson Mandela, Bill Clinton, Leonardo DiCaprio, Serena Williams and Hugh Jackman. In 1983 he performed an exercise that totally transformed his life. He set new goals and was determined not to accept anything less than what he was committing to as part of his process of boosting overall standards. He put all of his limiting beliefs aside and sat on a beach with a journal, where he wrote for 3 long hours straight. While he was brainstorming, he made a list of everything he could imagine himself doing, creating, having, being, experiencing, and contributing. He had set himself a time limit of one day to twenty years. He never stopped to think whether he could realistically accomplish those goals. He simply captured all ideas and possibilities that inspired him. He used that as a stepping stone, he went on to refine it, and in the next 6 months while he spent a lot of time traveling to different parts of Russia. He used that as a platform to further develop it over the course of the following six months, during which he traveled extensively around Russia.

While he was traveling, he started refining his goals on the back of the Russian map as he had nothing else to write on. He made a list of all his long-term goals for his spiritual, emotional, physical, mental, and financial destinies and started setting a series of benchmarks for each one working backward. For example, in order to achieve his top spiritual goal

10 years from now what he must do and what kind of person will he have to be for that to make it happen 9 years from now, 8 years from now and 7 years from now and so on until today. What Specific steps he could take currently that would lead him to his desired destination. On that day he set specific goals for what kind of a girl he wanted as his life partner. He went into great mental, emotional, spiritual, and physical detail about her. He gave a description of his family, work, home, and so forth.

When Life magazine visited him a year and a half later, they conducted an interview with him to find out how he had changed his life so drastically. It was astonishing to see how many of his written goals he'd accomplished when he pulled out his map to display them all. He had actually married the woman he had described. He had discovered and acquired the home he had envisioned, right down to the third floor office in the castle's turret overlooking the water. When he first wrote the objectives down, he had no assurances that they will be achieved. However, he had been willing to amend judgment for a short period of time to make it work.

This is an inspiring story where he literally creates the destiny, he wants by setting standards behind an old Russian map, which is how he now has more than 105 companies across the world and does revenues of over 5 billion dollars every year. For more than 37 years more than 50 million people in more than 100 countries across the globe have benefited with his generosity and transformational power that has impacted with his teachings on peak performance and personal development.

Our outputs determine our results. The world we live in is full of expectations, competition, balance and growth and the results we receive are never as good as the outcome.

What we often get from life is :

Expectation	Reality
Poor Job = Poor Results	Poor job = Negative Results
Good Job = Good Results	Good Job = Poor Results
Excellent Job = Excellent Results	Excellent Job = Good Results
Outstanding Job = Outstanding Results	Outstanding Job = Excellent Results

Poor Job: Poor work is not rewarded poorly. It gives negative results. A poor job is equal to getting downsized. Pain and negative outcome are the result of poor work.

Good Job: When you do a good job you get poor results. You are doing well at work, and you are overweight, stressed and lack social connections is ultimately poor results.

Excellent Job: When you do an excellent job the results you get are good. It occurs when every aspect of your life is under control and running smoothly.

Outstanding Job: Slightly above excellent is outstanding. When you are better than excellent and that's when your rewards are way higher than excellent.

It's not a skills difference, it's a psychological difference, a standard difference. You are aware of the outstanding qualities you possess, yet often, a voice may enter your head and say things that will make you doubt yourself. You need to transform that voice inside of you from one that terrifies and depresses you into one that gives you strength and motivation. You just have to tap that part of yourself. Just the way you build a muscle, you must keep practicing and working on it until it becomes second nature to you if you want to move to the next level.

Aligning Habits to Your Standards and Goals

It's crucial to establish habits that support the standards in addition to setting goals and holding yourself to a high level. As standards and objectives can only be met by implementation, you must begin committing to daily routines.

For instance, if you want to drop 30 pounds, you must establish daily routines for your exercise and food. The goals are accomplished during the process. Although having goals and standards to guide you is always a good idea, only sticking to the process consistently will help you reach your objective.

Many people make the error of putting more emphasis on the outcome than on the process. The desired outcome will materialize only when you are persistent in the habit you establish and maintain.

2. Changing Your Limiting Beliefs

Un-conscious beliefs are driving us every day. We hold opinions about relationships, wealth, career, health, and everything for that matter. As a result, the same set of emotions get triggered from our library of experiences and similar events keep happening in our life. As long as the same set of beliefs are being operated, we won't see changes happening. To change the situations in life we must begin absorbing new beliefs and eliminating outdated ones just like a tree sheds its old leaves in order to modify the situation in our lives.

Steven Kotler was a journalist in the early days of his career, and he was always on the lookout to share interesting stories. Space travel was very popular at that time, and NASA used to spend billions on rockets that could only launch once and never be utilized again. At that time Peter Diamandis who was the founder of X Prize had put up a 10million dollar prize for the first firm, team or an individual who could develop a reusable spaceship and can fly twice in space. That's when Steven came across this and wrote his first big National article about Peter Diamandis. Peter was a visionary who wanted to make space travel affordable for the general people and create reusable spaceships unlike the ones by NASA. This sector involved only the big players like big corporations and the big governments. Steven then began to discuss about this contest with NASA, aircraft manufacturing companies and engineers of such companies. Everyone offered the same response, claiming, "it's going to cost tens and billions of dollars to pull it off and would need thousands of engineers to make it happen, and mentioned it's impossible to accomplish X Prize for various reasons".

8 Years later a man named Burt Rutan won the X prize. Did it really cost billions of dollars to make? No, it took $25,000 only. Did it take thousands of engineers to build it? No, just required a 30-person crew. Here, Peter and Burt Rutan's team used the strength of faith to achieve the seemingly impossible. They refused to fall for the limiting beliefs that leading players in the same industry held. They did not shatter their beliefs and succumb to the limiting beliefs of others. They only kept believing that it was possible and kept going, to finally make it happen and create a revolution on the planet. Positive belief systems are

the common denominator in all achievements, from ground-breaking innovations to modest victories.

Exercise:

For anything that you want to manifest you can do an exercise that lets you overcome limiting beliefs, self-doubt and other negative thoughts that spiral you down. Ask yourself the below two questions.

Why it is possible?

Why do you deserve it?

When you do this exercise, you will realize that your attention is now directed towards empowering beliefs that we can cultivate. You can open new possibilities by replacing old, restricting thoughts and beliefs.

3. Game Plan

A game plan is nothing but a strategy. Strategy is like a recipe for making something. Anyone and everyone can use it. Once you have the strategy you can achieve all your goals in terms of finance, health, relationships and, all the other areas you desire. You just must follow the recipe to make it happen. Then once you understand the game plan you keep getting better at implementing it. There is a strategy for everything whether you want to advance in your career or have a fulfilling relationship, from making a deal for your company to developing six-pack abs.

A true story of a chiropractor who wanted to start a business in a US town.

The chiropractic association turned down his request to set up a clinic stating that the area already had more than enough chiropractors and didn't require anymore. But he just didn't buy no for an answer. He went outside and put a pin on the map where he wanted his office. For 6 months he went door to door and politely ask questions to these residents. He would ask them questions about will this be the ideal location to put up his office? Would they be willing to visit if he kept his home open for visits? What time frames are ideal for them? Where should he advertise? And so forth. One of the homes even gunned him down because they thought he was a hitman. He went on numerous adventures.

When he finally started his business, he had already visited about 12500 houses and spoke to 6500 households who were available at home at his time of visit. He finally opened his office in the same spot in a town that didn't need a chiropractor. In his first year, he made over a million dollars. He set up 6-7 more centers around California. While he launched his practise with a boom, even established chiropractors in that area weren't doing as much business.

This chiropractor used a strategy which no one else considered. He combined relentless enthusiasm with a strategy for success.

Jack Canfield had a student who had made 10 million dollars in 1yr on eBay selling pool tables and he never even graduated college.

By selling his pool table on eBay, Mr. Canfield's Student earned 600 dollars for his grandfather in a single day. That gave him plenty of motivation, and he later began searching for other pool tables in neighbourhoods and other locations where individuals were selling their unused units. Then he began importing pool tables and started selling them, finally earning over $10 million annually. Shouldn't we ask ourselves if he can do it why can't we?

These are just some simple strategies used by people to make a living. There is a way to apply strategies for every area of your life. You just need to find the means to make it happen. Whenever I feel I'm lagging in any area of my life, I just look back on this one aspect and evaluate if I'm using the right strategy. I immediately revamp or change my strategy. Many people do things accidentally, however with the right strategies you can implement them consciously.

4. Good Relationships: No Road is Long with Good Company

The Harvard Study of Adult Development conducted an intriguing study on 724 participants, who were examined from their teenage to their old age for 75 years. A psychiatrist by the name of Robert Waldinger shared the findings of this study and it was phenomenal. One of the longest studies on adult life ever conducted with fruitful results is this one. Each of these participants came from a diverse background and grew up to be having different professions like factory workers, lawyers, bricklayers, doctors, and even the president of the United States. The study revealed that the reason for one's happiness and health was not hard work, wealth, being famous, or any of the things people think of. The study of 75 years of research done with tens and thousands of papers and so much data collected revealed that the number one reason for one's happiness and health was good relationships.

3 Big Lessons Learned about Relationships from this Study Were:

1. **Social connections are good for us and that loneliness kills—**

   People who are socially more connected with family, friends, and community are happier, healthier, and live longer. They have a greater sense of purpose and stronger mental and emotional states.

2. **The quality of our relationships matters —**

   We could experience loneliness in a marriage or be lonely in a crowd. Living amidst conflict is bad for health. Whereas living in a good warm relationship is protective.

3. **Beneficial for Overall Health —**

   Good relationships protect our body and especially our brains which is one of the most vital organs for humans. Those who had good relationships and were secure about counting on their partners or friends or their community had better memories and had their brains functioning way better than those who had issues of trust and lack of commitment.

Chapter 6

Systems and Tools for Living

All successful people have some game-changing habits that are a reason for their success. However, no habit should be carried out subconsciously because doing so turns you into a robot. As humans, we are empowered to do things consciously and with full awareness. Rather than emphasizing the outcome or goal, it's best to set habits. Your habits will help you reach your goals. Shedding your old habits and instilling new ones can be challenging in the start as your body and mind are accustomed to certain patterns and suddenly, they find it too overwhelming to undergo a big change. To ensure a smooth transition, it is therefore essential we introduce new habits gradually. This makes it easier to adopt a new habit without having to start over.

If you are used to waking up at 8 am, start by waking up at 7.50 and then 7.40 and so on, gradually lowering the time each day. This is a sustainable way to change your habit. One may not be able to start waking up at 5 am every day immediately but with little effort every day there will be progress daily and one can get there and sustain. Only setting visionary goals is not going to get you to them. The only difference between someone who sets goals and achieves them vs someone who doesn't achieve them are the daily habits, systems and behaviours they follow consistently. The one who takes action, and sets daily habits and systems is the one who can attain their goals.

Cold Water Showers

Celebrities and billionaires like Bill Gates, Madonna, Lady Gaga, Liam Neeson, Katharine Hepburn, Miranda Kerr, Kate Moss, and so many others take cold water showers. Do you think they don't have access to hot water?

I've been a person who would never compromise on taking a hot shower. Even in peak summers when it's 40 degrees Celsius I used to take hot water showers. That's the level of conditioning I had, and cold waters were something that used to make me very uncomfortable. When I began my transformation journey one thing I learned was that to make progress we have to rewire our brains and break the old conditioning. For new results, need to start taking new actions. I knew so many successful people who would shower in cold water and I wanted to do the same, but I just did not have the courage for it especially when you have access to hot water 24/7.

So, I decided to do something about my habit of hot water showers and was thinking of ways to break this pattern of fear and discomfort with cold waters. I attended a summit where I got the opportunity to learn from Laura Hof the daughter of the most famous and renowned coach in the World "Wim Hof" also known as the Iceman. This man has over 26 World records for climbing Everest Base camp in shorts and without oxygen, a record in Guinness for the longest Ice bath for over 1hr 52 mins, and many more. It was overwhelming for me to learn from his daughter the breathwork and ice bath methods. I had the biggest fear of cold waters however I understood how our body and mind can be trained with the assistance of our breath. Laura assisted me to enter in a tub full of ice, which initially appeared to me as my deathbed. But eventually, I hauled the best state in me and got myself submerged in these large blocks of ice. I had to intensely focus on my breath and take long inhalations and exhalations. So, when you control your breath your mind and body also come into control. Our body has the mechanism and the intelligence to adjust to the temperature, however, we must keep our breath relaxed.

Even as a beginner I managed to complete the full duration of the stipulated 2mins. This moment was not just a breakthrough for me but also a moment of pride as I had conquered one of my biggest fears. Since then, I made a conscious decision to only take cold water showers. I trained my mind that when I can do an ice bath, I can take cold water showers too. Besides, I told myself all the amazing things that come with cold water showers. Until today I feel uncomfortable at times but that is only for the initial few seconds. I have primed my mind for no compromise. Also, when you start your day by doing something uncomfortable you are not only creating new neural pathways in your brain but also ready to take on bigger challenges over the day. We must become comfortable dealing with uncomfortable situations for our growth. This practice has given me so much control over my mind and body.

Benefits of Cold-Water Showers:

Coldwater showers can increase the dopamine levels in your brain by 250%.

They help you have glowing skin and hair.

They help increase Oxygen intake, heart rate and alertness.

Increased circulation.

Increases Immunity and more.

In addition to these physical benefits, they also build you mentally and emotionally. Taking cold water showers makes you uncomfortable. It pushes you to step outside of your comfort zone first thing in the morning making you more resilient to handle more challenges and more uncertainty. People are able to cope with more challenging situations like starting a business or experiencing ups and downs in daily life.

Exercise: Start taking a shower with lukewarm water and slowly bring it down to cold water.

The Power of Meditation

Meditation has been perceived as something which should only be practiced when you are on a break or on a retreat or if you are emotionally and mentally injured. It is regarded as something that cannot be done in a hectic schedule. It is not considered as being of high priority as most people are still not clear about its significance. I have lived in the ashrams and have experienced a monk lifestyle to finally understand that when we silence our mind, we can experience life or the soul within. People who lead busy lives need meditation even more considering their minds are "on" all the time.

Although meditation has ample benefits, the core essence is to connect with the divine which resides within you. It's to establish a connection with the life force or the soul that resides within you that has purity, peace, knowledge, love, joy, bliss, and power. Our ability to experience these qualities is increased only when we quieten our minds. Our mind and body are tools for this soul. However, most people are considering their mind and body as themselves and get deeply identified with them. This is making them restricted and constrained to a limited dimension of energy whereas we can access an unlimited dimension.

For us to experience the soul within, we must address the excess activity of the mind. The thoughts and activity of the mind are like the clouds and the sun is like the soul just as an analogy. So, when there is activity of thoughts, we are not able to witness our soul. It's like the clouds are blocking the sun. That doesn't mean the sun doesn't exist.

When we are in stillness without any thoughts, we experience our soul. It's like the sky is clear and we can clearly experience the sun.

This also allows us to experience the true nature of our soul. The more we keep touching this space the more we head towards strengthening our inner life and start experiencing its true nature.

We have lost touch with life itself due to social media, news, cultural conditioning, politics, lifestyle, collecting wealth and assets that keep our minds distracted and busy. Therefore, it makes utmost sense to practice meditation, especially when you start your day or just before going to bed. If you are trying to manifest something you desire then there are numerous guided visualization meditations, theta healing meditations, and many others which are readily available online.

I have experienced incredible results with the help of Raageshwari Loomba's Theta healing meditation (Guided meditation for Manifestation and overall wellbeing) where I have manifested exactly what I desired. With the tremendous meditations and practises of Sadhguru (Isha), which have greatly aided me, I have had wonderful outcomes.

There are plenty of resources and guidance available online but it's important to start. Initially, I began to meditate for 10 minutes a day and I used to keep track of whether it was helping me. And after a few months, I realised I was able to do yoga better, had better concentration, I was performing better with less efforts, had greater sense of awareness and aliveness. I was much calmer than before, and I could manage issues more thoughtfully. I realised if 10 minutes a day can make such an impact then I ought to increase this healthy practice. Now I do it for at least 1 hour a day and it's become a lifestyle. However, these benefits are just subtle benefits in the real world. It's like when you're building a muscle you don't work out for one day and expect to have muscles, right? You keep working on it and make it a lifestyle to have long term growth. Once you make it a habit you start enjoying the process. You will see results once you begin to follow the process. It doesn't matter who is doing it, everyone can see results with it. Regardless of who performs it, everyone can see and experience the outcomes. Anything that can be powerfully established in the mind can be manifested in the physical world.

Exercise: As a beginner, it is best to start with Ana Pana Sati a breath awareness meditation. Start with 5 minutes every day and progressively increase it. Over time, you will start enjoying the whole meditation process. Your ability to use your mind and body gets significantly enhanced with meditation.

Yogic Diet for Optimum Performance — Mitahara in Yogic Sciences

As per Yogic sciences, it's best to have a controlled or balanced diet which is known as Mitahara. In this you consume only ½ of your stomach with food, ¼ with water and ¼ is empty. This is to facilitate good digestion in the body. In the Mitahara concept, fresh, vital and sattvic foods should be consumed and one should avoid the consumption of stale, tamasic, and impure food. Tamasic in the sense that it needs to be consumed within 2 hours from preparation. After 2 hours of preparation the food starts gathering inertia and starts becoming Tamasic. Tamasic food when consumed reduces the aliveness in the system.

70% of our body is water, that's almost 2/3 of our body. Our goal is to make the food that we eat become a part of us at the earliest. Alkaline foods are majorly water-based, and they are highly recommended for optimum functioning of our body and mind. Alkaline foods alter the Ph value or the acid level in your body, improve well-being, manage weight, and help you combat cancer. Humans are anatomically herbivorous creatures. The intestines in our body are of the same length as that of the herbivorous animals. Our jaws and teeth are also of similar nature. The acids in our stomachs are not as strong as that of carnivorous animals. Although we can make our way with all kinds of vegetarian and non-vegetarian food, but if you want to perform in optimal states vegetarian food is what we have been designed for. I used to eat meat until the time I started understanding more about its implications on the human system. Meat takes around 40hrs to digest and is acidic in nature. So, when you eat meat the acid level in the body increases and your digestive system is working extra hard to digest this food. Due to its complexity and difficulty in digestion, the process of digestion is greatly burdened. The digestion of alkaline foods can take 2-4 hours to digest. As they are water-based it consumes almost 1/10th the amount of time compared to meat.

Imagine leaving a piece of meat outside while the temperature is 37degrees Celsius. How long do you think it will take for it to get spoilt? According to reports, after 2 hours the bacteria start multiplying at a rapid rate and in about 8-10 hours may be potent enough to spread odour and begin to rot. Imagine this meat in your stomach. In your stomach it's always summer, what do you expect would happen if it's in there without getting digested? Because of the length of the intestines, food travels slowly through them and complete its process. Bacterial activity increases, raising the risk of food poisoning.

The gastrointestinal system secretes gastric acids which support the digestion process that help in breaking down the food you consume. When you consume meat or have a poor lifestyle or with processed food choices the body tends to lose its ph balance with excess acid leading to acidity or other gastric issues.

Acidic foods leave a residue after they digest which is called acid ash and is a primary contributor to many stomach issues. Alkaline food also leaves ash however it is protective and not harmful like acidic ash. Some of the food sources which leave acidic ash are protein, phosphate, and sulphur.

Tamasic Foods: Meat, poultry, fish, onions, garlic, mushrooms, stale food and fermented foods like vinegar, bread, pastries, cakes, and alcohol.

Sattvic Foods: Fresh fruits, whole grains, seeds, sprouted seeds, honey, ghee, nuts, legumes, and vegetables.

Some Healthy Foods:

Green leafy veggies

Spinach, lettuce, kale, celery, cabbage, collard, and mustard green are very rich in vitamin A, B, E, folic acid and minerals iron, calcium and phosphorus. These are very essential for having a dynamic immune system and have proper function of our overall physical system.

Cauliflower and broccoli contain high volumes of vitamins A, C, k and folate and phytochemicals plant compounds that are treasured in dropping soreness and preventing the threat of cancer.

Citrus Fruits

Lemon, sweet lime and oranges are rich in vitamin C, which helps to cleanse our system and provide relief from heartburn and acidity.

Nuts

Almonds, walnuts, and cashews regulate blood sugar spikes, improve heart health and manage weight.

Root vegetables

Sweet potato, beets, radish, turnips, and carrots are an excellent source of dietary fibre that helps to boost gut good bacteria, diminish high levels of cholesterol and minimize the risk of various chronic diseases.

So, it's fantastic to include some alkaline foods in your meals if you've been chowing down on processed foods, meat, and junk.

In my experience Alkaline foods have helped my body and mind perform better. In addition, I was able to lose the necessary weight—from 78 kg to 65 kg—to reach my desired weight and my immunity has been rock solid with the help of this diet. Mitahara is a terrific diet lifestyle to follow which has plenty of benefits and alkaline diets are ideal for people who don't engage in a lot of physical activities. If you are a sportsman, then you might wish to consult a dietician. However, alkaline foods are just amazing if you want your brain and intellect to work at their best.

Drinking-Water

By the time we wake up after a long night of sleep, our bodies have lost a lot of water. If we start our day by drinking 500ml of water, it hydrates both our body and brain. Our brain is mostly water, and it consumes 20% of the energy in our bodies. So, for optimal brain function, a sattvic and alkaline diet, as well as plenty of water, are essential.

Mindful Eating

The food that we consume is energy and this energy can be contaminated with negative thoughts and emotions from its surroundings. Both food and water have memories, and they store the energy of their surroundings. When we consume this food, we are consuming vibrational energies as well. Becoming conscious of these energies is one aspect of mindful eating. That's why it's advised to pray before you eat and bless the food. If you go to South India there are people who still consecrate their food with water before they eat. Eating this food in the right state and consciously is what we need to do. What we are consuming is life and we need to be consious as this life becomes a part of us when we consume it.

When we are watching something and eating, the content of what we are watching can trigger certain emotions in us and that can lead to improper digestion and excess eating as well.

The Magic of Gratitude

"The more grateful I am, the more beauty I see." – Mary Davis

Gratitude means thankfulness, appreciation, and gratefulness. We count our agonies carefully but accept our blessings without any gratification. At every moment in our life, we have so much to be thankful for, however, we often take things for granted. We feel that to be grateful there should be something worth being grateful for. But you can find gratitude in every small thing. When I realised the power of gratitude, I made a commitment to make it one of my core values.

Every 10 seconds a kid dies of hunger and over 9 million people die each year due to starvation. If we had a meal today, then we should be grateful for it. We might not be grateful for having a horrible boss but think about those who don't even have a job and are struggling for one. We might not be grateful for our small apartments but over a billion people lack proper housing and shelter.

One of the most profound epiphanies came from reading Dr John. D. Martini's "The Gratitude Effect", where he asks us to look back in our lives and see aspects that we wished were different and asked us to reflect on them. Growing up I always thought my dad was strict, insensitive, and nagging. I used to wish I had a father like that of my friend. My friend's father was always carefree, pampering, and easy going. I used to tell myself that if I ever become a father I will never be like my dad, that's the level of resentment I had towards my dad. But when I reflect on my life today, I realise I would never trade my life for that of my friend. I am able to go this far is because of my dad, who helped me become who I am today. Had he been a different person I wouldn't be who I am today. I started being grateful for having him the way he is. His nagging nature increased my level of patience and tolerance and made me the calm person that I am today. His insensitive behaviour made me a much stronger man to deal with situations and hardships. I became a go-getter because of his habit of not spoon-feeding me and forcing me to accomplish things on my own. When I became aware of these facts, I literally had tears of joy and gratitude. I now view dad with the highest respect and gratitude because I recognize his significant contribution to everything that I am today.

I have been practicing two-morning appreciation rituals "Thanking the universe with a smile for having me alive as soon as I wake up. Given that nearly two people die every second, being alive should be a cause for celebration. We should be grateful that it's not us or the ones within our friends and family who passed away. I then start feeling grateful for everything I have, my family, friends, assets, employees, and so on. There is a proverb that goes "What you appreciate, appreciates." When you are in the state of gratitude you are in a positively elevated state, and it is not possible to have any other states to co-exist with this state. When you are feeling thankful, you cannot be angry. When you are in gratitude, you can't experience jealousy, stress, resentment, misery, pain, anxiety, depression, fear, or guilt.

I compiled a list of things to be grateful for after my mother passed suddenly from a cardiac attack while she was fighting cancer. As I started listing, her passing changed from being a sad tragedy to something I could cherish.

My list appeared to be as follows:

"I am so grateful that my mom got relieved from all kinds of suffering due to cancer"

"I am so grateful that my mom had such a peaceful demise at her own home on the bed and in my arms"

"I am so grateful that I got to spend so much time with her during her last months"

"I am so grateful that I and my sister could pamper her as her son and daughter"

"I am so grateful that we were able to give her the best of healthcare treatment".

"I am so grateful that she was with her entire family the last 6 months"

"I am so grateful that this event made me become so close to my sister"

"I am so grateful that her funeral and all rituals happened effortlessly in spite of Covid lockdowns"

"I am so grateful that she was able to leave her body at ease"

I could have been lonely, sad, angry, or regretful. However, none of these factors could have changed the incident. When I chose to be grateful, I started feeling it was meant to happen and it happened for the best. I had a ton of reasons to be grateful at the time I prepared the list. So, no matter what situation you are in when you see it as a divine intervention at play and accept it with gratitude you will not be afflicted by pain.

Dr. Joe Vitale (popular author) shared one of the most moving stories of gratitude about a time in his life when things were chaotic. He was completely broke, living in squalor, and was trying everything in his life, but nothing really worked. He didn't drink or use drugs. No bad things but life was just a mess at that time. He had ambitious ambitions and used to attend free seminars and events to learn new things. But could just see nothing was working his way. One day, he discovered the value of gratitude and he reasoned to himself, "Why not try it?" One fine day while he was at his place and all he had was a pencil and he was wondering if he didn't even have anything to be grateful for, and how can he be grateful? However, being grateful doesn't work that way. You must be grateful right away. Since he didn't have anything at his place and was sitting there with a book and a pencil, he decided to undertake an exercise and began listing the things he could be grateful for, including his pencil. Even though he was not grateful for the pencil he said I'm grateful for this because "I can write a grocery list." "I can write a suicide note." He continued to say things like this and as time went, his responses rose in quality. He then said he can write a great novel or write a movie script or a song or a manifesto that would transform the world. He became incredibly excited as he spoke and even began to feel some degree of gratitude. Within minutes, the young man experienced a transition from a sceptical, irate to someone who was grateful and appreciative for life. He was angry at the start of the exercise, and he didn't do it out of gratitude but in fact to prove it wrong.

But when he started, he began to feel gratitude and nothing actually changed at that moment. He was still broken, alone, and living in a squalor but something within him had changed. Since then, he started seeing possibilities in everything and long story short he wrote a book that was published. Now he is one of the world's most renowned authors and is popularly known for appearing in the documentary "The Secret". He has the story of rags to riches with the simple practice of gratitude.

He mentions regardless of the circumstances in life, nothing matters. We must be appreciative for life at the present moment.

Gratitude Exercise:

Write down 10 things you are grateful for or just achknowledge it in your mind. Do this every day. Some of your points might repeat every day but it's alright. It's about getting into the attitude of gratitude.

Power of Knowledge and Loss of Ignorance

In an interview, Bill Gates was asked "If you could have any one superpower, what would it be and why?" His answer was, "Being able to read super-fast" He went on to explain how important it is to be a lifelong learner. And reading is such a core part of that lifelong learning. We are living in the digital information age, and we have access to millions of sources to get information to learn and grow our knowledge. Websites like Udemy, Mind Valley, and Coursera have thousands of topics for free and paid content by some of the best industry experts. Apps like Audible and Storytel have audiobooks that are so convenient for you to listen to, while you are traveling or while you are engaged in any other activity where you may simultaneously listen to these audiobooks.

Learning something new creates fresh synaptic connections between our neurons. It is just like the way we build muscle. We cannot expect biceps overnight. We have to keep working on it consistently.

Being Conscious

How conscious we are is how much of our destiny we determine. Most of us have been driven by our lifestyles into mental patterns. This creates a cycle of the same thoughts, words, emotions, and actions. We have unconscious behaviours governing the way we feel, think and act. If we are subject to this program, then it's not really our free will. We are just being stuck in a loop of patterns. The only way we can break these patterns is with awareness. That is nothing but being conscious.

When you have this compulsive urge of checking your cell phone hold yourself back. This is one of the ways of breaking compulsive behaviours. The next time you feel like eating that cheesecake, you wait. When you wait and reflect on the urge, that's when you are connecting with yourself and not with the compulsive behaviour and pattern of the mind. We can break unconscious patterns by bringing awareness and being conscious of the urge of the mind. We have to be the driver of our minds and not the other way around. Most people are suffering from their own mind that has turned against them. When we are conscious our ability to experience life is enhanced and we can experience elevated states of consciousness naturally. Simple practices that can be started with complete awareness can be taking a shower, defecating, and eating food. Over time we can start with more advanced practices to bring breath awareness, body and mind awareness in our day to day lives. Being aware of our breath, our physical body, our thoughts, and our emotions can give us complete control over our lives and can help us build a conscious life.

Self-Discovery and Development with Journaling

Journaling is one common ritual recommended by all leading transformational-coaches of the world. I learned about Journaling from the extremely well-known Robin Sharma who's best known to be the author of the book "The Monk who sold his Ferrari". When journaling, it is advised that you write with a pen rather than taking notes on your phone or laptop.

Science has proven that writing has its benefits that override other ways of journaling. Some ideas for you to begin writing are:

- 10 things you are grateful for that day

- Any disheartening or emotional experience that occurred in the past.

- Anything that is bothering you or has been constantly on your mind.

- Write down the goals you wish to accomplish.

- Write affirmations, incantations, or statements.

Here are Some Reasons why you Should Start Journaling Today-

It Helps you to be Grateful

Our brains have been wired to see negativity in things. Therefore, it has become important to start practicing deliberate gratitude and build on that muscle to a point where we start seeing everything is happening for us and not against us. The happiest people deliberately set aside time to celebrate gratitude.

It Helps Release Low Energy Emotions

If we have any unresolved emotional experiences lingering in our subconscious mind, they are consuming a tremendous amount of energy. There is an amazing phenomenon that happens when we write it out. Because you are reliving the experience it passes from the subconscious mind to the conscious mind. The emotions come out of the experience and flow through our hands and spill onto the sheet of paper. Writing allows us to express ourselves fully and makes us feel much lighter.

Consolidates your thinking

We often have a lot going on in our minds. When we put things in writing, we give them more attention and awareness in our lives. It aids in clearing our minds of mental clutter and organizing our thoughts.

Relive Cherished Moments

When we record precious moments, we may look back on them whenever we want to relive the memories.

We frequently have things for which we may be grateful today, but with time we forget to be thankful for them. When these items are captured, we can use them to replay special moments whenever we want.

Cultivates Hope

The toughest times often make us the most resilient. We should perceive possibilities for self-mastery and hope during difficult circumstances.

Increases Retention

Writing helps memories become more solid and simpler to hold onto.

They help you program your thoughts, actions, and behaviour.

Autobiography

Writing experiences about your life story turns it into an autobiography.

Journaling Exercise:

Buy a journal and start writing today.

Embracing Self Love

If an acquaintance deems you ugly, you feel hurt and start second-guessing yourself, then you covertly believe you are unattractive. Your feelings about yourself have surfaced instead of their words, which is what has disturbed you. For Instance the same acquaintance calls you bald when you are not, that wouldn't impact you as you know that's not true. But when someone called you ugly you felt it because somewhere in your beliefs there is a doubt within that exists which makes you feel "you are ugly". This is not an external problem but an internal problem. You won't believe even supermodels who look gorgeous and handsome have self-doubt and can feel they are ugly or not good enough.

"I am not what I think I am, and I am not what you think I am. I am what I think you think I am." – Charles Cooley

This means that our perception of how other people view us affects us.

This is a narrative we run in our minds all the time and is purely our own creation. You could be making this self-sabotaging or self-empowering. What we believe others feel or think about us often has an impact on how we feel about ourselves. And we make decisions based on how we believe others see us.

Since childhood, we are being conditioned to believe that who we are depends upon what our family, friends or society think or do. Our past experiences have shaped the way we feel or think. With Self-love you can accept who you are and be compassionate for yourself as the way you are is complete, beautiful and the way it's supposed to be. It's about embracing your unique look and nature because no two people are the same in the world. It's about truly accepting who you are and the way you appear and shaping your personality to fit that.

As a child, if you were told not to play sports even though you really loved them, then your personality was being shaped by someone else. That goes with so many of your habits, values, and your personality.

Therefore, we alter our true personalities and true nature by refusing to embrace who we truly are and by making room for what other people want. So, recognising and appreciating our genuine selves is what self-love is all about.

Self-love is about accepting ourselves the way we are and not being influenced by what society thinks about us or what society expects us to do. Why should we hide our true nature simply because it does not fit in the scheme of someone else?

Exercises:

1. Practise in front of the mirror to look in your eyes and say "I love You" again and again. Looking in the eyes makes us aware and helps reprogram the mind and can also aid in healing any old scars.

2. Put up a poster with the words "I am enough" in your room.

   Since childhood, we have been looking for social approval and frequently judge ourselves based on how we believe others might see us, which is frequently a negative perception. This kind of affirmation of "I am Enough" will strengthen your conviction that you are perfect just the way you are.

Segment Intending

Segment intending is a powerful exercise that helps you construct your future using your intentions and visualisation. When you set an intention, you are activating the RAS (Reticular activating system) in your brain that looks for associations that are significant to you. When you buy a new car, you notice there are more of the same car on the road. This is because your brain has associated with it and the focus and attention towards those cars have increased.

So, I use segment intending to picture

How my overall day would look like.

How my business will appear.

How I will approach my workout.

I even utilize it before calls, games, meetings, or any other occasion, and I visualize a successful outcome before I begin the activity. This allows me to focus on the things that matter to me the most.

Also intentions have such power, they often come true far too quickly if you have a strong frame of mind. You may have observed that when you set an intention for something you want and are in a particularly good state of mind, it often manifests swiftly and easily. While occasionally you just can't get it no matter how hard you try.

Everything depends on the mental condition in which the intentions are expressed. Always make sure your intentions are in higher states, such as gratitude, love, happiness, etc.

Blessed is He Who Plants Trees Under whose Shade He Will Never Sit

"I cried because I had no shoes until I met a man who had no feet".

– Helen Keller

One of the most inspiring stories of selfless giving, compassion and sharing is that of Sindhutai Sapkal. Her life started as an unwanted child followed by an abusive husband. She was married at a very tender age of 10 while her husband was 30 years old. Her spouse used to frequently beat and savagely mistreat her.

Finally, when she was 20 years old and nine months pregnant, her husband left her. She had to cut the umbilical cord herself with a sharp stone next to her after giving birth alone in a cowshed. She mustered the strength to travel miles and go to her mother however she refused to take her home.

These incidents left her so devastated that she considered suicide. However, she gathered courage and inspiration to battle the situation. She lived at the railway station and begged to feed her child and herself. Soon she realized the plight of other orphan kids and thought to raise them as well, despite the fact that she herself had little to offer.

She used to beg all day to adopt more and more kids. Over time her work started getting traction and people started supporting her. Because of her speaking skills, she frequently received invitations to speak at events, which allowed her to earn a living for her kids. She devoted her entire life to the welfare of children and gave them love, food and education. She arose through time and became a mother to over 1400 orphans. Her children have grown up and became doctors, lawyers, IT engineers and more. Sindhutai continued to work toward her goal of being a mother to orphans up until the time of her death and used to give lectures to make a living. Sindhutai rose to prominence in the Indian community as a result of her frequent speaking engagements, and she received over 500 awards for her noble deeds.

She was a classic example who gave unconditionally and in return received abundantly from her children and society.

Our wealth grows as we give. There is an old proverb "Give and you shall receive." This is actually true, and I tested these laws. At first, I found it difficult to accept this. We always prioritise wanting above providing. I was never the kind of person who could just give away my hard-earned money for charity or for the underprivileged. I have always been a helpful kind of person and if anyone wanted a favour, I would be more than willing to do it for any stranger but donating money was something I was still not in terms with. That's because I have had many limiting beliefs about money. It is the law of giving that I wanted to put to test. I was like Jo from the book "Go Giver" who wanted to test the law and see if it actually works. Millions of people have tried and tested this, and it actually works. I started donating to charitable organisations with good intentions while keeping an awareness if something proportionate to it is coming to me from someplace but not keeping any expectations. You won't believe it, but I started noticing that magical experiences began to occur. I just realised the synchronicities were so insane that it just couldn't be a coincidence.

Strangers began to assist me at random.

I began receiving business recommendations from unexpected individuals.

I began to get unanticipated funds from several sources.

Apparently, this law works with whatever you give.

So, if you give love, you receive love.

If you donate money, you receive money.

If you give hatred, you get back hatred.

It is not necessary that if you give love to someone, you might receive it from the same person. It could come to you from anyone else. However, you do attract the energy you put forth.

Forgiveness is the Attribute of the Strong

When a certain incident occurs and we believe that the other person did not act appropriately, we harm ourselves. We cause ourselves suffering by rationalising that the other person's actions were wrong and that we would never be able to forgive them. Now, it's possible that the other person has no remorse since they never thought they had done anything wrong.

The victim in this situation, however, is the one who is clinging to the hurt and is unwilling to forgive, not the one who committed the deed. Whether the perpetrator is accountable for their actions or not, the one who suffers is the one who clings to the pain. I had never realised I had stored such energies of pain, anger, and discomfort within me just by holding on to things others had done to me. The effects of me holding on to other people's acts were on myself, not them. I didn't accept what they did until I realised that forgiveness is a means of releasing yourself from pain. This allowed me to forgive them and release the pain, anger, and discomfort within me. When we hold the other person responsible for our pain, we justify the other person's actions and hold their actions responsible for the pain we feel. We expect them to apologise before we can forgive them or let go of our feelings. We end up holding on to those awful feelings up until the point where the other person offers a sincere apology. The more we think about it we keep increasing those negative energies within us which also manifest in various physical ailments.

Only humans can store and carry such feelings for days, months, years or even decades. Often there is a probability that the other won't apologise, however you can still be relieved from the pain by simply forgiving them even without the apology. Because we are the ones holding on to the pain and when we forgive the other person and bless them with good intentions, we are not only relieving ourselves from the pain we are holding but also sending out positive energies to the other person. When you send positive energies out, the first person to experience it is ourselves. The same is true about bad thoughts and energies that we have sent forth. Therefore, the best thing we can do in response to someone's actions that have hurt, angered, or disappointed us is to first forgive them to let go of the negative energies we are harbouring, and then bless them in order to radiate the positive energies that we experience and that are sent to them as well. Forgiving someone is more for our personal benefit than it is for the other person specifically.

So, the next time don't ever think of saying "I'm never going to forgive that person" because you will be the one suffering. Forgive and bless!

Magical Hours of the Day

"We first make our habits then the habits make us." – John Dryden

The initial 2 hours of your day are the most important hours that set the tone of the day. Not only are you in a relaxed state when you wake up but also priming your mind becomes easy. Some of the most successful people in the world have adopted strong early morning routines and habits that shape their life into who they are. They use their doorway to their subconscious and the morning cosmic energy in the best way possible. Waking up and checking your phone is one of the worst ways to start your morning as you are flooding your subconscious mind with content that is not required to be embedded deep within. Instead, it should be used to install something that can be really empowering your emotions and your mind.

The following are some of the top methods to start your mornings, as advised by some of the world's most successful people:

1. **Drinking 500 ml of water** – Your body is 2/3rd water and when you wake up you are dehydrated. Water helps you hydrate your brain and body.

2. **Being Grateful for 5 things** – The state of gratitude is a highly elevated state and counting your blessings sets the right tone for the day.

3. **Visualization meditation** – Morning is the best time to program your subconscious. It is best to visualise the future outcome as if it is true in the present and truly feel them.

4. **Making your bed** – You start your day by accomplishing a task. Gives you enough motivation to start the day on a positive note.

5. **Cold Water Shower:** Besides the many benefits of cold water showers, it trains your mind to start your day with challenges and dealing with uncomfortable situations. It increases the dopamine in the brain by 250%.

6. **Breath works** – You can practice Fluttering, Wim Hof Method, and Pranayama to name a few.

7. **Anapana Sati Meditation** – Observing Inhalation and Exhalation of your breath. This is a powerful practice to sharpen your mind and bring it under control.

8. **Remembering your dreams** – Helps you exercise your brain in the morning

9. **Doing Physical Exercise** – Get your heart rate up and your blood flowing for your body and mind to function better.

10. **Reading** – Read something positive that will help you elevate yourself emotionally, intellectually, and mentally. Avoid the news channels as you end up consuming a lot of negativities.

11. **Journaling** – Journaling is a great practice that helps you mentally, emotionally, and intellectually.

The Manifestation Formula

We know that the brain is goal-seeking. If you give your brain any target it will go for it. How does a GPS work? If you have a map and if you want to get somewhere you have to put the destination, right? So, you must know where you are and where you want to go. When you visualize this, you should be creating an image of them and the feeling of it. Get a feel of the house you want to buy and place a picture in front of you on a vision board. Get the test drive of the BMW you always wished to buy and then stick a picture of it. This way you have also had the experience of that feeling and with you seeing it every day your actions will lead you there. Paste it wherever you will see it. Make it very clear to your brain.

Nasa did a study that you can completely rewire your brain by creating new neural patterns in your brain in 30 days of uninterrupted visualization, affirmations and with positive thinking you can completely rewire it. You cannot skip a day. If you do 10 days and skip one day and do it, it's day 1 again.

30 Days Principle to Manifest any Goal

1. **Clarity and Ask**: Make a clear list of your desires before addressing the universe, God, or whatever other name you choose to use for this existing greater force.

2. **Be Descriptive:** Write a detailed description of what this desire looks like and feels like. It's like writing a PO (Purchase Order) to God. It's important to be as descriptive as possible.

3. **Believe in it and Apply Visualization:** You must have a strong belief that what you have asked for with deep emotions is going to manifest. Use visualizations at least twice a day especially right after waking up and before going to bed as those are the times our mind is highly receptive to programming. Imagine it with feelings as though it were already real.

4. **Take Actions:** Without taking action on your desire, you cannot expect it to happen. There must be an action plan for achieving what you desire. Every other factor influences your decisions.

5. **Surrender:** Once you have taken the desired actions, surrender to the higher power and forget about it. Just like when you plant a seed you don't keep thinking about whether it will grow or not. You keep taking care of the manure, sunlight and water for the seed. The rest will take care of itself if you simply concentrate on the process.

Never Give Up on Your Dream

Jack Canfield Manifestation Story

Jack Canfield's 1st book Chicken Soup for the Soul was rejected by 144 publishers. Comments like "nobody reads short stories" and other disparaging remarks drove them away. Jack and Mark visited numerous publishers before one ultimately agreed to publish them and predicted a sales volume of 20,000 copies. In response, they stated that selling 20,000 copies was not something they were interested in doing because their aim went far beyond selling a million volumes. The publisher laughed at them and said, "That's not realistic," in response and declared them to be insane. As business owners, Jack and Mark understood what it meant to run a successful business. In brief, they have adhered to the Rule of 5 since the book was published.

Every day they took 5 actionable steps. After 14 months it came on the bestseller list.

The book spent the next 3.5 years as the No. 1 Best Seller. Then, the fact that 7 Chicken Soup for the Soul books were on the New York Times list, broke a Guinness World Record. Therefore, keep pursuing your goals!

One can create their life consciously based on what they truly believe is impactful and that gives them happiness and fulfilment.

The Inspiring Story of Chad in the River Clean Up Mission

Chad Pregracke grew up in East Moline, Illinois, where the Mississippi River was in his backyard. As a teenager, he worked as a commercial diver and noticed the heaps of debris in the well-known canal waterway — one that supplies drinking water to millions of people across the United States. He was astonished to learn that people would dump tires, cars, trucks, fridges, etc. He then started using his boat to clean the river. Then things got to the point where he needed a crane and other equipment for greater debris, which would cost money. So, he opened the yellow pages and started dialling. He dialled the Alcoa firm, telling the receptionist that he wanted to talk with the "top person." He was so naïve and innocent. He simply said to the front desk clerk, "I am cleaning the Mississippi river and I need money". The receptionist got him funding for $5,000 USD after noticing his enthusiasm for this worthwhile endeavour. This boosted his morale and then he approached more businesses and was successful in obtaining additional money from the next one. He raised 2.4 million dollars over the course of the following two years and persuaded 5 CEOs to serve on the board of directors for his cause.

Chapter 7

Conscious Living

Happiness in the Now

Once we realise that we are all mortal we begin acting in ways that bring us happiness and fulfilment. Although we all know about our mortality but we are ignorant of it since we have taken life for granted. We might all pass away at any time, but we rarely take drastic action unless something major occurs. Near-death incident survivors have undergone significant life changes. If you were given a second chance at life, would you spend it on meaningless activities? If you knew you were going to pass away soon, would you continue to be doing what you're doing? You never plan to retire if you are working at something you love. Who would want to stop doing something they find enjoyable? When we engage in activities that can satisfy our souls, we can all feel content and happy.

Our soul is constantly sending us signs however we have just shattered it with our own psychological creations. We have been extending this state by continually looking for anything that we believe will bring us happiness. If I receive that promotion, I will be happy, when I purchase that car I will be delighted. When I own that home, I will be satisfied. When I retire, I will be content. But once you have it, the happiness just vanishes. They were simply our materialistic or goal-oriented desires that we believed will bring us the greatest levels of happiness.

The "If-Then" model of happiness has a flaw.

A very interesting study was done by Ken Honda, a Wealth Expert who has interviewed various millionaires and billionaires. He questioned a millionaire," if he felt wealthy during an interview with him". No, the millionaire said, adding that he would consider himself wealthy if he had ten million. When he asked someone with $10 million if he felt rich and the response was "No", and he desired a private jet to feel rich. When he interviewed someone who owned a private jet if he felt rich, the man responded, "No," adding that his private jet is a 6-seater and I want a bigger one." My jet seems small around the other private jets he said. The point here is no amount of money will give happiness and largely we have designed our lives towards accumulating financial wealth.

Happiness should not be tied to any goals or outcomes. We must find happiness in the present. We must get better at enjoying the moment. According to research, happiness in the now increases success and productivity. Look at some of the wealthy people in the world and ask yourselves are they really happy? We wonder why they commit suicide, and presume they had a fantastic life filled with fame, success, money, and all the other worldly possessions. They have everything that money can possibly buy and yet a monk who has no physical possessions seems happier. One could wonder, why are the wealthiest people on earth so greedy? They already have so much, we wonder what else someone can possibly need. Humans have a constant desire for more. Even though we only have 2 people living in a 5BHK villa we would want a bigger one. For a billionaire, billions could be less, and they would like trillions more. This longing for more drives us humans. This longing can be put to our best use by understanding how we can impact this world in the best possible way and how we can live our lives to the fullest.

Higher Purpose and Values

Some billionaires felt they could retire after selling their businesses for billions of dollars, but as soon as they did, they started using drugs and alcohol, which led to their complete downfall. They lost their purpose and the joy of fulfilment that they used to get when they were doing something meaningful and engaged in significant work. No matter how wealthy we are, a higher purpose must always drive our lives.

The more we connect our lives with this higher purpose, the more we will be able to feel fulfilled and operate at a much higher frequency to give optimum results. I stayed in the ashrams and learned from the teachings of Sadhguru and various other spiritual masters. One thing I learned was, "there is absolutely no purpose for life. Life is a "happening" and we are here to experience it". We are just manifestations of the same consciousness being expressed in different forms. If we are getting distracted from life itself, then it's our failure. When I say life here, I don't mean your career, relationships, wealth, etc. Im referring to the life process that is throbbing within you. Which is your awareness or consciousness.

We all can live in a way that can be positively impactful. Often, we go above and beyond what we would do for ourselves to help others. If it were your kids, parents, girlfriend, or pals, you would do something you wouldn't do for yourself. That gives people joy and that is why you may notice people feel more fulfilled when they are a host than being a guest.

Some individuals think they don't know how to find out their highest values. Our soul is constantly giving us signs, but we always end up making decisions that are influenced by societal norms, our friends and families, the media, our traditions, and other things. Then we start convincing ourselves that this is what we must do and then we become so entrenched in that to an extent where we make it challenging to emerge out of it. We get influenced by society thinking, everyone is chasing this may be if I get there, I will get the happiness and fulfilment. However, a lot of people know what gives them happiness and fulfilment but don't pursue in that direction for various reasons. We need to start making conscious decisions and really ask ourselves that if I'm doing this will it be significant enough even after 20 years or 30 years or when you are on your deathbed? Will you look back and wish you had done something meaningful with your life instead of something pointless? Would you prefer to have an impactful life that made a difference in people's lives?

Being on a Mission – Legacy and Impact

One of the exercises I learnt from Steven Kotler, who is regarded as one of the world's most renowned experts on ultimate human performance enabled me to experience a significant shift. We are all aware that our time on this earth is limited, but our legacy may last forever. Take a look at Mahatma Gandhi, Nelson Mandela, Mother Teresa, Osho and so many more. These are individuals who, long after their passing, left a legacy.

Imagining Your Funeral

Imagine your funeral is taking place right now. What do you believe your influence to be on people until today? What do you think your impact has been on people up to this point? How many individuals will attend your funeral? What will people say about you? What are their opinions about you? What personality type will others use to describe you? How many people will this news make sad? Have you left behind any legacy? How many people did you influence?

Your impact need not be on a global level but what was the impact you had on your maid, your watchman, your neighbors, friends, colleagues, relatives, and society as a whole?

Which would you choose: leaving a large financial legacy or having a significant social impact?

There are numerous ways to influence and affect lives and to alter someone's course in life. A sweet compliment can leave a lasting impression in someone's heart for a lifetime. Small positive teachings could financially change a family's status. Your financial assistance to the poor may enable you to provide them with food.

"People will remember you, for the values you had, for the happiness you brought, for the good deeds you did, for the revolution you created, for the disruption you were, for the energy you had, for the good words you spoke, for the mind-set you had and above all for the lives you touched." – **Lisa Nichols**

The Inspiring Story of Terry Fox

Terry Fox, as he was known by Terrence Stanley, was a 21-year-old Canadian athlete, Humanitarian and Cancer Activist. Terry's right leg had to be amputated and despite that in 1980 he set forth on a journey to cover the East to West of Canada to raise funds for Cancer research by the name of The Marathon of Hope. He ran 5373 kilometers in 143 days and finally he was forced to stop running as cancer had spread in his lungs. Nine months later, he passed away. However, he had created a global long-lasting legacy. The annual Terry Fox Run started in the year 1981 and has grown exponentially to have millions of participants from over 60 nations making it the World's biggest one-day event, By the end of January 2018, "The Cancer Marathon Fund Raiser" had raised over 750 million dollars.

Fox won the 1980 Lou Marsh Award as the nation's top sportsman and was named Canada's Newsmaker of the Year in both 1980 and 1981. He is regarded as a national hero and has had numerous buildings, statues, highways, and parks named in his honor around the nation. He was also the youngest person to ever be made a Companion of the Order of Canada.

Terry knew he had a finite life to live and wanted to leave a legacy that not many people would be willing to attempt. His influence has endured for four decades, and even young children find inspiration in him. Numerous marathons throughout the world still bear his name. Although we are aware of our limited lifespan, we mistakenly believe only other individuals pass away. Someday, both you and I shall pass away. That might occur right now as well. But we put off or kill our dreams, desires, ambitions, and passions for yet another day, finally see them completely being vaporised.

Elon Musk had once tweeted "Many people will panic to find a charger before their phone dies. But won't panic to find a plan before their dream dies." Unfortunately, this is the ugly truth.

Due to fear, procrastination, lack of clarity, lack of self-worth, low self-esteem, and self-doubt, our passions and dreams frequently fade away and die.

How often have you wanted to do something, but your cynical thoughts kept getting in the way, stopping you in your tracks and keeping you from taking any action? Or someone said something demotivating and you give up on it.

Now let's look at this from a hypothetical situation and see.

Ask yourself if you were to live only for a month would you still do the work that you are currently doing?

Let's take my example.

The legacy I want to leave is of someone who was

- Loving

- Always making a difference in other people's lives

- Was grateful for everything he had

- Was youthful, playful and an avid explorer to learn and travel

- Was spiritual

- Was always happy and spreading happiness

Our life can be consciously designed when we bring awareness and make changes. It's important to discover our values and our liking to deep dive into them and create the life we desire. Till then it's important to explore things with an open mind. Let's not blindly become victims to social ideologies and beliefs about the way every aspect of life needs to be. It's important to "Be" and discover the real "You".

Each one of us on this planet is unique and each one can shine and unleash their true potential that can serve the planet in some impactful way.

Finding True Purpose Consciously

"I think everybody should get rich and famous and do everything they ever dreamed of so they can see that it's not the answer." – Jim Carrey

The thing you might be chasing could be just a mirage of happiness. I had figured out the money and time systems, but I was still in search of my ultimate happiness, influence, and fulfilment. I began to question whether I was acting in my financial interests. Am I acting in a certain way because society, my parents, or other family members want me to? Do I want to make an impact by doing this? Am I being deceived by what success looks like in the modern world?

Are my visions and goals truly mine or are they strongly influenced by someone else?

This led me to explore a lot about myself and required a lot of inner reflection. I completed a Vishen Lakhiani exercise in 2019 from the "Be Extraordinary" course. In the following activity, we are asked to list the items we want in response to the following questions.

1. What is it that you want to experience in life?

2. How is it that you want to grow to make those experiences come to life?

3. How do you want to contribute and impact this world?

I got clarity on what could be truly fulfilling for me and impactful for the people. It's only when we write and reflect deep within ourselves that we tend to find clarity.

While doing the introspection and trying to find my true passion and fulfillment I realized

I love traveling

I love meeting new people

I enjoy learning new concepts from experts and implementing them

I want to make a considerable impact in the lives of others by helping them transform

I cherish connections with influential people

I love being on a transformational journey to evolve and grow as a person

I adore teaching and having a positive influence on people's life.

This led me to my purpose of helping people break compulsive behaviours and to start living conscious lives. This inspired me to start the venture Conscious Living Mission, and I am on a mission to persuade people to adopt conscious living to drastically alter their quality of life.

I am now on a mission to assist working professionals in achieving fulfilment, peak performance, happiness, clarity, sense of belonging which will result in an internal change. This developed only after extensive critical reflection, introspection, and clarity. I spent months dwelling in ashrams and what I learned from every spiritual leader is that the divine exists within you and you can access the divine whenever you wish to. You don't have to go anywhere to seek it but just go within. For years I never understood what it meant "To go Within". I always just found it like a cool statement. However only experientially do I understand how profound that experience is. The experience that I once had cannot be compared to any drug, an orgasm, or the experience of peeing when your bladder is about to explode. This experience was so divine and cannot be expressed in words and is something which each one should experience themselves. It happened to me at a time when I was meditating and I left my mind, body and emotions aside and was in total stillness. That is when the magic happened. I went into a state of bliss which was something I had never experienced in my life. I took no action, and it happened. I spoke to my master about the incident and that's when he told me that's an experience of touching your true being.

Sadhguru and various other spiritual teachings mention that when you set aside your thoughts and emotions you become receptive to the grace of any person, teacher, or the divine. We have trouble keeping our minds still. Our thoughts are the cause of our lack of clarity. It's like a mirror being smudged with dirt that doesn't allow us to see ourselves clearly. When we empty our minds from thoughts we get connected to our true selves and our level of perception towards life gets immensely enhanced. The life that we are is like a drop in the ocean. So, the drop in the ocean is also the ocean. We are composed of the same elements as everything else in the cosmos. The same substance makes up the planets, stars, animals, and humans. When we consider ourselves a part of the universe, we realise that we are also the universe and that we are plentiful beings with limitless potential. We can function in higher realms of consciousness and perception when our soul is the driver and commanding the mind and body.

Ancient eastern disciplines like yoga, vipassana, meditation, and kriyas all emerged as a means of transcending our bodies and mind. Spirituality is a doorway for our overall well-being and to create conscious lives. It makes no sense to complicate the process of our survival to the point where, despite our comfort, wealth, and possessions, we are unhappy and engaged in a never-ending search for meaning. Over this journey, we might lose the essence of experiencing life which is the biggest phenomenon. We will never be content with materialistic desires and hence it is important we explore the dimension of the non-physical which is limitless. It's in the boundless that lies the ultimate scope of exploration.

"May we all get a taste of our true being that is of love, purity, wisdom, peace, joy, bliss and power." – Anand Narayanan

Next Steps:

If you have enjoyed this book and if you want to deep dive into transformation and personal growth in all aspects of your life, then you can enroll in our Conscious Living Mentorship Program that helps you transform your life.

We take a comprehensive approach to consider your body, mind, emotions, and life energies, unlike other transformation organizations. With the goal of facilitating online and in-person retreats and workshops, Conscious Living collaborates with some of the top teachers, therapists, psychologists and facilitators in the world.

Conscious Living: https://www.consciouslivingmission.com/

About the Author

Anand is a successful serial entrepreneur, public speaker, yoga instructor and coach for conscious living for working professionals. He has diversified from artificial intelligence in IT to human intelligence in spirituality to solve mental health challenges. He has more than a decade of experience in the transformation industry. For numerous blue chip and Fortune 500 businesses, he has directly collaborated with world leaders, educators, and renowned mentors to accomplish tech and management transformations. He holds two degrees, including an MBA from MIT. He has training in yoga from one of the top universities in the world, Kaivalyadham, and he engages in traditional spiritual practices every day. He has over 15,000 students across 148 countries learning from his Online courses.

His Ventures:

Anika Technologies: https://www.anikatechnologies.com/

Conscious Living: https://www.consciouslivingmission.com/